The Day of The Lord
A Series of Sermons for the Last Days

Evangelist Martha P. Davis

The Day of The Lord

A Series of Sermons for the Last Days

Evangelist Martha P. Davis

ISBN: 978-1-965943-06-9

Dedication

Evangelist Martha P. Davis was a woman after God's own heart—a servant, teacher, missionary, and faithful steward of the Gospel who lived a life devoted to the Lord Jesus Christ. Although she went home to be with the Lord in 2022, her legacy continues to inspire and transform lives today. Evangelist Davis's unwavering dedication to teaching holiness, purity, and a life chastened before God was evident in every aspect of her ministry. She not only taught these principles but exemplified them in her daily walk, leaving an undeniable mark on those who were blessed to encounter her ministry.

Her life was one of worship, wholly surrendered to the call of Christ. She tirelessly carried the message of salvation across continents, traveling to Africa, Europe, Greece, Israel, the Philippines, and throughout the United States. Her passion for missions and her love for people led to thousands coming to know Jesus as their personal Savior. One of her most impactful platforms was her radio broadcast, which reached listeners across the United States and many parts of Africa and Europe. Through her anointed preaching, Evangelist Davis brought the light of the gospel to countless hearts and homes.

This book is a testament to her life's work and a tribute to the power of God's Word as proclaimed through her ministry. Within these pages, you will find a collection of some of the sermons that aired on her beloved radio show. These messages are timeless, filled with profound insights, fervent prayer, and a deep love for the Lord.

As you read these sermons, may you be encouraged, challenged, and drawn closer to our Lord Jesus Christ. Evangelist Martha P. Davis may no longer walk amongst us, but her words, filled with the power of the Holy Spirit, continue to speak life, hope, and salvation. May her legacy inspire you to live a life of holiness and devotion, just as she so faithfully demonstrated.

To God be the glory for the life and ministry of Evangelist Martha P. Davis

Foreword

The times we live in are filled with uncertainty, chaos, and a growing disregard for truth. As we witness the world slipping further into darkness, many are asking: *What does the future hold?* The answer lies within the pages of Scripture, where God has made it clear that a day is coming—a day of reckoning, a day of divine justice, *The Day of the Lord.*

Throughout history, the warnings of God's coming judgment have echoed through the voices of His prophets, apostles, and faithful servants. Yet, as Jesus foretold, many have turned a blind eye, scoffing at the idea that He will return. The world continues to spiral into moral decay, corruption is rampant, and deception is at an all-time high. But the truth remains: the Word of God will not fail, and the prophecies written in the Book of Revelation will come to pass. The signs are all around us, those with eyes to see and ears to hear must take heed.

In *The Day of the Lord*, Evangelist Martha P. Davis boldly proclaims the message of the last days as revealed in the Holy Scriptures. She takes us through the prophetic timeline of the rise of the Antichrist, the reign of evil upon the earth, and the great suffering that will come upon the nations. But this book is not written to invoke fear—it is written to awaken and prepare the people of God. Now more than ever, believers must be spiritually ready, standing firm in their faith, and walking in obedience to the Lord's commands.

With urgency and clarity, this book outlines the steps necessary to ensure that you are ready for Christ's return. It serves as both a warning and a guide, reminding us that while the world will fall into deeper darkness, the light of Christ will shine ever brighter for those who remain faithful. Jesus will open up the sky on *The Day of the Lord*, descending with the armies of heaven to execute judgment upon the wicked and to establish His righteous reign. The question is, will you be among those who are found worthy to escape the coming wrath?

This is not just another book—it is a prophetic message, a call to action, and a guide for all who seek to be ready when the skies break open, and Jesus Christ returns in power and glory. Do not take these warnings lightly. Let these words stir your spirit, awaken your faith, and lead you closer to the One who holds eternity in His hands.

The time is short. The day is near. Are you prepared?

G.K. Montilla

Index

Isaiah's Prophesy

Praise God, surely God is good, and He is greatly to be praised in His people everywhere. The word of God says, *let everything that hath breath praise the Lord.*

But He is worthy to be praised forever, throughout all eternity, beginning now. God wants to be praised and He is worthy of the praises of men. Let everything that hath breath praise the Lord.

God is good to us. I can never, never cease to say God is good to us because we live of His goodness every day. It was God's goodness that woke us up this morning. And I'm sure everyone can say that it is true, amen. I'll be ministering today from the book of Isaiah chapter 2. You that have your Bibles, please turn to Isaiah chapter 2.

Let us pray.

Father, in the authority of Thy name and in the name of Thy son, Jesus, we come boldly to the throne of grace this day. We need Your help to help us. We need Your grace, O God. We need Thy mercies. We need Thy abundant grace to help us today. In this hour in which we live, we need You as never before.

And we're engaging Thy help right now. Lord, as Your word comes forth by the power and the unction of the Holy Ghost, let it come forth bringing down yokes and fetters that have been bound in the hearts and in the minds of the people. Thy word is power indeed.

Thy word is Thine anointed power. Glory to God. And send forth Thy word to open the eyes of the blind and to unstop the deaf ears. Glory to God. Allow, O God, Thy word to penetrate in the depth of the heart and soul of man. Father, show forth Thy excellent praise.

Watch upon Your word and let it fall on good ground. We ask it in the precious name of Thy son, Jesus. Destroy the works of the enemy that he has planted in the minds and in the hearts of humanity. And let the word of God come forth unhindered.

Bind the forces of hell. We bind in Jesus' name this day the forces of hell that will fight against Your word, that will steal Your word as it comes forth from the lives and the minds of the people for which You are sending it to perform.

Thy word, Lord, is a lamp unto our feet and a light unto our pathway. It's not what man wants to hear, It's what You know we have need of. Thy word, O God, is Thy testimony. Send forth Thy word and the power of the Holy Ghost in Jesus' authoritative name we pray, amen and amen.

Isaiah chapter 2.

> *The word that Isaiah, the son of Amos, saw concerning Judah and Jerusalem. And it shall come to pass in the last days that the mountain of the Lord's house shall be established in the top of the mountains and shall be exalted above the hills and all nations shall flow unto it.*

Isaiah starts reading, starts writing, speaking through the unction of the Holy Spirit, the prophet of God. Moved by the Holy Spirit to write the word that Isaiah, the son of

Amos saw, concerning Judah and Jerusalem. You see, the word of God is power. What God speaks is power.

Not one word is unpowered that God speaks. Every word that He says has deep meaning. And this is what He's saying.

He's talking about the mountain of the Lord's house. How it should be established in the top of the mountains. And shall be exalted above the hills and all nations shall flow unto it. He's talking about the thousand year reign of the Lord Jesus Christ. We know Jerusalem is the center of the world. Israel, God has placed in the center of all nations of the world... the wisdom of God.

The marvelous wisdom of God. And God loves Israel. He's given Israel to those that He promised. He promised Abraham. Everyone is calling themselves the son of Abraham, that Abraham is their father. He is the father or the patriarch of faith, yes, indeed he is. And we are the seed of Abraham worldwide, if we have accepted Christ Jesus by faith. Hallelujah.

Even the Gentiles that are born again by the Spirit of God are the seed of Abraham, because Abraham was a man of faith. And God promised him that He would give him the seed as the sand of the sea that cannot be numbered.

And this He has done. So, by right, when one calls themselves the seed of Abraham. We cannot call ourselves of Abraham's seed unless we are born again by the Spirit of God into the kingdom of God through Jesus Christ. It's the only way... It's the only way.

God planted Israel to be of the holy city. The nation Israel, God planted a beautiful city there called Jerusalem. It is upon the hills. It is a high hill, the city of Jerusalem.

And God planted it there. And no matter what man has tried to do to destroy Jerusalem. And many wars, many kings and kingdoms have come against that natural city to destroy it, but God has kept that city intact. Even though other places have laid dormant, God has kept the city of Jerusalem intact. Praise God in the highest.

It's for a purpose. And it's for God's future plans, as well as the plans that are being carried out today concerning Jerusalem. In verse 3, I won't go any further into that just now, but I will come back later on in our study. But in the third verse, He says,

> *And many people shall go and say, come ye and let us go up to the mountain of the Lord,*

meaning the city of Jerusalem.

> *Let us go up to the mountain of the Lord, to the house of the God of Jacob. And He will teach us of His ways. And we will walk in His paths. For out of Zion shall go forth the law and the word of the Lord from Jerusalem.*

The word of the Lord from Jerusalem. Praise God in the highest. And we, around the world, around this globe called the world, can say we have heard the truth out of Jerusalem.

Praise God. Jesus Christ, the way, the truth, and the life, gave His life a ransom in Jerusalem that all the world might be saved. What a powerful promise that God brought forth when Jesus Christ went into Jerusalem to lay down His life for all mankind. Everywhere, throughout all the world, throughout all nations, Jesus Christ came speaking the word of God the Father. What a mighty Savior. And this is why He is called the word, the living word.

For He spoke the word of God from Jerusalem and round about Jerusalem. Praise His holy name. And when it was time for Him to lay down His life, to give His life a ransom for all mankind, He made His way back to Jerusalem to die there. To die there, because the word had already gone forth through the prophets of old. It was in the scriptures that Jesus Christ would give His life a ransom for us all. Praise God and thank God for Jesus.

He did it from Jerusalem. He did it from Jerusalem. It was God's plan from the beginning that Jesus Christ would lay down His life from Jerusalem, Hallelujah.

In that thousand year reign, there's a time coming when Jesus Christ will come back to this earth the second time. And when He comes, He's going to put down all rule and all authority of man.

And He's going to take His rightful place. And He will rule with a rod of iron. And He's going to bring nations, nationalities up to Jerusalem to hear the word of the Lord. That they might learn who He is and the purpose of the Father and of new Jerusalem that shall be coming out of the heavens to dwell on earth.

God is going to do a mighty work during that thousand year reign. During the time that Jesus Christ will take over the rule of all the world. He's going to rule from the capital of the world, Jerusalem... Jerusalem! Praise His holy name.

He says in verse four,

> *And He shall judge among the nations and shall rebuke many people and they shall beat their swords into plowshares and their spears into pruning hooks. Nations shall not lift up sword against nation. Neither shall they learn war anymore. O house of Jacob, come ye and let us walk in the light of the Lord.*

What is the light? Jesus Christ. He speaks the truth, He speaks the truth. He speaks the word of God the Father. And the word is truth.

> *Therefore, thou hast forsaken thy people, the house of Jacob, because they be replenished from the east and are soothsayers like the Philistines. And they please themselves in the children of strangers.*

The Lord is upset because Jacob, whom God has chosen to walk in this beautiful path of righteousness, chose to walk contrary to the word of God that came out from Jerusalem.

Actually, it came out from God in heaven to Jerusalem through Jesus Christ. And the Lord is seeing all the marvelous things that He had planned for Jacob because of Abraham. Abraham, Isaac, Jacob.

And because they did not carry out God's beautiful plan to obey His word, to obey that that He has spoken to them, the Lord, the word of God says, the Lord,

> *Therefore, thou hast forsaken thy people, the house of Jacob, because they replenished from the east*

and are soothsayers like the Philistines. And they
please themselves in the children of strangers.

They refuse to walk after God. They chose to walk after
soothsayers, according to the ninth chapter of
Deuteronomy, it should not be... It's the work of the devil
to follow after magicians, astrologers, soothsayers. They
perform necromancy, calling out to the dead, supposedly
loved ones.

It's all the work of the devil. It's all the work of the enemy
to lead the people into darkness and to take on the form and
the ways of strangers instead of the way of the Lord. God's
way is right, His path is righteousness. And God doesn't
deal with the devil. God has nothing to do with the devil.

He's the enemy of God and He's the enemy of all souls of
men. And the people that God raised up to do His will, to
walk in the path of righteousness, to walk in the light of the
truth, chose to abide in darkness and to take on the ways of
strangers whom God had forbidden that they go in and be
partaker thereof. He said,

> *Their land also is full of silver and gold. Neither is*
> *there any end of their treasures.*

They increased in riches, you see.

> *Their land is also full of horses. Neither is there any*
> *end of their chariots.*

Like today, plenty of cars everywhere.

> *Their land is full, also is full of idols. They worship*
> *the work of their own hands, that which their own*
> *fingers have made.*

Not bringing God glory, not giving the Lord the honor that's due unto Him.

> And the mean man bowed down and the great man humbled himself. Therefore, forgive them not.

God has turned against them because they turned against God. And these are the things that, these are the complaints that God has against the children of men. Because when God spread out the beautiful things in the earth, He did not long for the people to make idol gods out of His beautiful handiwork, His creation. No, that was not God's plan for humanity. God placed things in the earth that we might seek them out to the glory of God, to give God the glory.

Because He is the creator of all things. And instead of men giving God the glory, they take the glory upon themselves and make these things their own idols. Anything that you put before God is an idol. And He says, because of this, God shall pour out His wrath. God is looking at the ways of humanity. And what He sees is not pleasing at all in His sight.

We can't use the term, not altogether pleasing. No, it is not pleasing at all in the sight of God. And this is what He says. This is what Isaiah the prophet is saying. He is speaking, not of his time, not in the age that he lived. This is the Holy Spirit speaking through this prophet of God, Isaiah, of the last days.

And it's coming to that point now. He says,

> *Enter into the rock and hide thee in the dust for fear of the Lord and for the glory of His majesty. The lofty looks of men shall be humbled.*

That's the proud look of man.

*And the haughtiness of men shall be bowed down
and the Lord alone shall be exalted in that day.*

God alone. Now, it should be that way now, but God is
allowing man to make his choice. Even though He's
preaching the gospel through His servants, He's telling
mankind to surrender all to Him, to come in unto the ark of
safety and be saved, to be washed in the blood, get your
sins forgiven. This is the cry of God's heart today.

The dispensation of the gospel is being preached
throughout all the world that mankind will know what the
will of the Lord is.

But man chooses to be lofty in heart and haughty in spirit
and refuse to humble themselves before the mighty hand of
God and let their hearts and eye be made single before the
Lord of hosts. So, God sees that their day is coming. Their
calamity is coming. And He's prophesying through Isaiah
of that great day of calamity. It's called the great day of the
Lord or the day of the Lord. It means the vengeance of God
is coming.

And He is going to be like a madman when He begins to
pour out His wrath in the way that it's going to be poured
out. Nothing or no one is going to pacify Him until His
heart is satisfied because He knows the heart of man.

There is a remnant in this earth that is going to be saved
from the wrath of God. But the Word of God says the wrath
of God comes upon the children of disobedience. The Word
of God is warning people everywhere.

When God poured this in my spirit this morning to come and minister this over the air, bringing it to His people worldwide in every country that this handmaiden's voice is to be heard. And I am not alone. God has people that will speak His truth.

Our gospel is not accepted by most people. The truth is despised. Men is looking to themselves to have teachers to tickle their ears and tell them they are all right.

But I am here to be faithful to God and to be faithful to warn you to escape the wrath of God to come for it is coming precious souls. And the choice is ours. The choice of our destiny is ours.

We choose where we are going to live eternally. It's our choice. If we turn a deaf ear to God's pleadings, to His divine pleadings and to His warnings, that choice is ours. But one day we are going to pay for what we have chosen to be. We will pay. Glory to His name.

> *The lofty looks of men shall be humbled.*

I'll read this again.

> *And the haughtiness of men shall be bowed down and the Lord alone shall be exalted in that day. For the day of the Lord of hosts shall be upon everyone that is proud and lofty and upon everyone that is lifted up. And he shall be brought low.*

God is warning every person under the sun, i'll read it again.

> *For the day of the LORD of hosts shall be upon every one that is proud and lofty, and upon*

every one that is lifted up; and he shall be brought
low: and upon all the cedars of Lebanon, that
are high and lifted up, and upon all the oaks of
Bashan, and upon all the high mountains, and upon
all the hills that are lifted up, and upon every high
tower, and upon every fenced wall, and upon all the
ships of Tarshish, and upon all pleasant
pictures. And the loftiness of man shall be bowed
down, and the haughtiness of men shall be made
low: and the LORD alone shall be exalted in that
day.

Do you hear the prophecy of God? Do you hear the word of the Lord? Man can lift himself up and raise up his head and turn up his nose at the gospel and at the divine pleadings of the most high God. But God is saying, when I move against you, I am going to tear up everything that you ever praised, everything that you have ever loved. I am going to tear it asunder and I am going to bring it low.

Even though the beautiful trees and the ships, the chariots, even, God is saying he's going to bring it low, the souls of men, the haughtiness and the pride, God is going to break down and lay low. And he says, and the idols he shall utterly abolish. Verse 18, and the idols he shall utterly abolish.

What you have said in your heart upon now, God said he's going to destroy it all together. He's going to wipe it out all together.

And they shall go into the holes of the rocks and
into the caves of the earth for fear of the Lord and
for the glory of his majesty. When he ariseth to
shake terribly the earth.

11

God is waiting, he's waiting for you to humble yourself and come in unto the ark of safety. Jesus Christ is the ark of safety.

God is waiting for you to humble yourself and realize that you need the savior. The only savior that God has given to the children of men, his only begotten son. And I don't care who you are or what you are called by.

You need Jesus Christ. You're going to need him in the end. When God shakes terribly this earth with a power that comes only from God's mouth.

Glory to his name. You're going to need to know Jesus Christ as your personal savior, your friend, and your Lord, your strong and high tower. And if you don't know him, you're going to run to the rocks to hide you from the wrath of God, but it's not going to work.

He says,

> In that day a man shall cast his idols of silver, and his idols of gold, which they made each one for himself to worship, to the moles and to the bats; to go into the clefts of the rocks, and into the tops of the ragged rocks, for fear of the LORD, and for the glory of his majesty, when he ariseth to shake terribly the earth. Cease ye from man, whose breath is in his nostrils: for wherein is he to be accounted of?

What are you going to do when you choose your own way? In the end, you find yourself cast out from the presence of God and under his divine judgment forever. All your idols cannot save you in that day. It is time to come in to the Lord God Almighty, to the Son of God, Jesus Christ. He is that door. There is no other way. Hear the voice of God this day. I speak to you the word of God in power, in Jesus name. Amen.

Would You Die for Him?

God is good to us. I've always said and always will say as long as I live and have my being, God is good. He is good to the children of men, whether we belong to him or not. He is still good, and his word is good, all of God's word is good.

It's good to counsel our hearts, to show us the way that God would have us to go. It's good to know the mind and his mind is in the word. The word reveals what's on the mind of God.

So it's important for us to go into his word and to know without any doubt by his grace and power and by his divine revelation, amen, to know what thus said the Lord.

Last week, we started ministering on the topic, the day of the Lord. To me, this is one of the most important topics in the word of God, other than Christ Jesus coming and fulfilling that that God had moved upon the prophets of old to prophesy of the day of our redemption, that the Lord would redeem us by the shedding of his blood, giving us access to the throne of grace through him, only through him.

That is one marvelous thing that Christ Jesus has done. And all the world is able to benefit by this mighty work of salvation that Jesus Christ has accomplished for all mankind at Calvary. But Jesus Christ, when he comes again to the earth, he's not coming as the savior of all the world as he did of old... 2,000 years ago.

When Jesus comes back to this earth the second time, He's coming as the King of kings and Lord of lords, as we read to you. And I will read again on the behalf of those that maybe did not hear us in the last broadcast. In Isaiah chapter two, beginning at verse 10,

> *Enter into the rock and hide thee in the dust for fear of the Lord and for the glory of his majesty. The lofty looks of men shall be humbled and the haughtiness of men shall be bowed down and the Lord alone shall be exalted in that day.*

What day? The day of the Lord, when he comes to demonstrate in power and vengeance and wrath against those that have come against his beloved, meaning the children of Israel and the city of Jerusalem. As I said before, Israel and especially Jerusalem is set in the very center of the earth, of the earth, mind you, this is the wisdom of God. And God and God alone is going to set up rule in Jerusalem. I see men making plans and plans of falling through because man is imperfect.

And especially when their hearts are not going after the word of God to do things according to God's will, man will fail. In all their endeavors and in all of their meetings together, man will fail because God has a timetable. And God's timetable, what we're to look at is Jerusalem and Israel itself today.

And I want to read to you from the book of Acts, the seventh chapter of the book of Acts. This is when Stephen, the one that was martyred for speaking the truth to the Israelites of old. When the mighty move of the Holy Ghost was on the move and souls were being saved, there's always the enemy and his crowd, the devil and his crowd that will declare war against the truth, the things that God will speak and has spoken to mankind.

We don't make up these words. We go by the scriptures, because it's the word of God, the scripture is God's word. The Holy Bible is God's word. Many have fought and declared that it was written of man, but man is not perfect. The word of God is perfect. And everything that God has written in here, it's perfect.

There is no loopholes anywhere. But the only way we can understand what God is saying, we have to be born again. We have to know the mind of Christ Jesus. And it's given to us to know the mind of Christ. In the seventh chapter of Acts, Stephen is speaking on the behalf of God Almighty in the move of the Holy Spirit. He's speaking in the defense of the gospel.

He says, beginning at verse one,

> *Then said the high priest, are these things so?*

When Stephen is arrested, he's talking about the things of God over in the sixth chapter in the eighth verse,

> *And Stephen, full of faith and power, did great wonders and miracles among the people. Then there arose searching of the synagogue, which is called the synagogue of the Libertines and the Cyrenians, and Alexandrians and of them of Cilicia and of Asia, disputing with Stephen.*

And we have it today, people disputing the word of God.

But Stephen was full of the Holy Ghost and a man of great faith. So he's speaking God's word. And he says,

17

Then they suborned men, which said, We have heard him speak blasphemous words against Moses, and against God.

And they stirred up the people, and the elders, and the scribes, and came upon him, and caught him, and brought him to the council.

In other words, they arrested him because of the word of God that was spoken. Because man in his natural state of mind, and especially when he's full of the devil, the devil hates God's word.

When he's full of the devil, he is not going to hear the truth. Remember Pilate? He says, what is truth? And truth was standing right before him, humbled and meek, ready to go to the cross, even for him, even for Pilate, as well as the whole world. And in verse 15,

And all that sat in the council, looking stedfastly on him, saw his face as it had been the face of an angel.

Now we shall proceed in chapter seven.

Then said the high priest, are these things so?

In other words, did you speak blasphemy against Moses and the law? And he said,

Men, brethren,

this is Stephen answering,

Men, brethren, and fathers, hearken; The God of glory appeared unto our father Abraham, when he was in Mesopotamia, before he dwelt in Charran,

I looked up the word Charran, it's also called Haran. It's a city located in northern Mesopotamia, a branch of the Euphrates, to which Terah, the father of Abraham or Abram, immigrated with his family. And it's found in Genesis 11:31.

After his father's death, Abram departed from the city to go into the land of Canaan. So this is where Stephen is talking of,

> and said unto him, get thee out of thy country,

verse three,

> and from thy kindred, and come into the land which I shall shew thee. Then came he out of the land of the Chaldeans and dwelt in Sharon. And from this, when his father was dead, he removed him into this land wherein you now dwell,

in the land of Israel,

> And he gave him non-inheritance in it, no, not so much as to set his foot on: yet he promised that he would give it to him for a possession, and to his seed after him, when as yet he had no child.

You see the faith of God and Abram obeyed God. And it was counted unto him as righteousness because he believed and obeyed the voice of God.

> And God spake on this wise, That his seed should sojourn in a strange land; and that they should bring them into bondage, and entreat *them* evil four hundred years. And the nation to whom they shall

be in bondage will I judge, said God: and after that shall they come forth, and serve me in this place.

And he gave him the covenant of circumcision: and so *Abraham* begat Isaac, and circumcised him the eighth day; and Isaac *begat* Jacob; and Jacob *begat* the twelve patriarchs. *And the patriarchs moved with envy, sold Joseph into Egypt. They sold their brother into Egypt, but God was with him.*

And I like that, but God was with him.

Remember persecutions, but God being with us in the persecutions, taking us through the persecutions. This is how he dealt with Joseph

> *And delivered him out of all his afflictions and gave him favor and wisdom in the sight of Pharaoh, king of Egypt. And he made him governor over Egypt and all his house.*

God exalted him to a high place while still in Egypt, from prison to governor of all the land of Egypt.

> Now there came a dearth of all the land of Egypt and great affliction and our fathers found no sustenance. But when Jacob heard that there was corn in Egypt, he sent out our fathers first.

> *And at the second time Joseph was made known to his brethren; and Joseph's kindred was made known unto Pharaoh. Then sent Joseph, and called his father Jacob to him, and all his kindred, threescore and fifteen souls.*

So Stephen knows the history of the Jews and he's repeating this to those that have called him in to counsel. He is speaking the truth. He's giving them the history. He's giving them the background, which they well knew anyhow, but God is using Stephen for a purpose.

> *So Jacob went down into Egypt, and died, he, and our fathers, and were carried over into Sychem, and laid in the sepulchre that Abraham bought for a sum of money of the sons of Emmor the father of Sychem. But when the time of the promise drew nigh, which God had sworn to Abraham, the people grew and multiplied in Egypt, Till another king arose, which knew not Joseph.*

The Pharaoh that Joseph was raised up under to a high and lofty place in government died. And another Pharaoh took over and he didn't know Joseph.

> *The same dealt subtilly with our kindred, and evil entreated our fathers, so that they cast out their young children, to the end they might not live.*

> *In which time Moses was born, and was exceeding fair, and nourished up in his father's house three months: and when he was cast out, Pharaoh's daughter took him up, and nourished him for her own son. And Moses was learned in all the wisdom of the Egyptians.*

He was raised as an Egyptian from the time he was three months old until the age of 40 and was mighty in words and in deeds.

> *And when he was full 40 years old, it came into his heart to visit his brother and the children of Israel.*

At this point, he had learned that he was not truly an Egyptian, but his heritage was Jewish.

> *And seeing one of them suffer wrong, he defended him, and avenged him that was oppressed, and smote the Egyptian: for he supposed his brethren would have understood how that God by his hand would deliver them: but they understood not.*

They didn't realize that not only was he fair to look upon, he was also anointed. He was also chosen to do the will of God. It was foreordained to bring deliverance to the Jews that were in bondage down in Egypt, but they understood not.

> *And the next day he shewed himself unto them as they strove, and would have set them at one again, saying, Sirs, ye are brethren; why do ye wrong one to another?*

He sees two Israelites fighting one another. And this is what he said.

> *But he that did his neighbour wrong thrust him away, saying, Who made thee a ruler and a judge over us? Wilt thou kill me, as thou diddest the Egyptian yesterday? Then fled Moses at this saying, and was a stranger in the land of Madian, where he begat two sons.*

He ran away to stay alive.

> And when forty years were expired, there appeared to him in the wilderness of mount Sina an angel of the Lord in a flame of fire in a bush.

When Moses saw *it*, he wondered at the sight: and as he drew near to behold *it*, the voice of the Lord came unto him, *saying*, I *am* the God of thy fathers, the God of Abraham, and the God of Isaac, and the God of Jacob.

Then Moses trembled, and durst not behold. Then said the Lord to him, Put off thy shoes from thy feet: for the place where thou standest is holy ground.

I have seen, I have seen the affliction of my people which is in Egypt, and I have heard their groaning, and am come down to deliver them. And now come, I will send thee into Egypt.

This Moses whom they refused, saying, Who made thee a ruler and a judge? the same did God send to be a ruler and a deliverer by the hand of the angel which appeared to him in the bush.

They asked 40 years previously, who made thee a ruler and a judge? But God made him not only ruler and the ability to judge right from wrong, but also a mighty deliverer to deliver the children of Israel out from under bondage of Pharaoh down in Egypt.

He brought them out. After that, he had showed wonders and signs in the land of Egypt and in the Red Sea and in the wilderness 40 years. This is that Moses, which said unto the children of Israel, a prophet shall the Lord your God raise up unto you of your brethren, like unto me, him shall you hear.

I want to read this again, verse 37,

23

This is that Moses, which said unto the children of Israel, a prophet shall the Lord your God raise up unto you of your brethren, like unto me, him shall you hear.

In Acts the third chapter, beginning at verse 22,

For Moses truly said unto the fathers, A prophet shall the Lord your God raise up unto you of your brethren, like unto me; him shall ye hear in all things whatsoever he shall say unto you. And it shall come to pass, that every soul, which will not hear that prophet, shall be destroyed from among the people. Yea, and all the prophets from Samuel and those that follow after, as many as have spoken, have likewise foretold of these days.

Ye are the children of the prophets, and of the covenant which God made with our fathers, saying unto Abraham, And in thy seed shall all the kindreds of the earth be blessed. Unto you first God, having raised up his Son Jesus, sent him to bless you, in turning away every one of you from his iniquities.

Praise God in the highest. That was the purpose of God sending Jesus in the likeness of human flesh amongst the Jews. As a Jew, that Jesus came to his own first. Praise God. He came to be the Savior. He came to be the Savior of the soul and to write each one's name in the Lamb's book of life that would receive him. But when Jesus comes again, he is coming as a mighty conqueror.

I want to continue to read in Acts chapter 7. I'll read 39 again.

To whom our fathers would not obey, but thrust him
from them, and in their hearts turned back again
into Egypt.

In their hearts, mind you, they did not go physically back to
Egypt at that time, but in their hearts they turned again back
into Egypt.

Saying unto Aaron, Make us gods to go before us:
for as for this Moses, which brought us out of the
land of Egypt, we wot not what is become of him.

This is when Moses was up in Mount Sinai, getting,
hearing the voice of God and getting instructions for the
children of Israel to live by until a greater deliverer came
forth, receiving the Ten Commandments.

And while the children of Israel were in the wilderness
waiting for Moses to come down, and Moses stayed so
long, their hearts fainted. And so they appealed to Aaron,
the high priest, to make another god for them. And we
know about the fatted calf, we know about the golden calf.

Verse 41,

And they made a calf in those days, and offered
sacrifice unto the idol and rejoiced in the works of
their own hands.

Sounds familiar today, doesn't it?

Then God turned and gave them up to worship the
host of heaven; as it is written in the book of the
prophets, O ye house of Israel, have ye offered to
me slain beasts and sacrifices. By the space of forty
years in the wilderness? Yea, ye took up the

tabernacle of Moloch, And the star of your god Remphan, Figures which ye made to worship them: And I will carry you away beyond Babylon.

Our fathers had the tabernacle of witness in the wilderness, as he had appointed, speaking unto Moses, that he should make it according to the fashion that he had seen.

Which also our fathers that came after brought in with Jesus into the possession of the Gentiles, whom God drave out before the face of our fathers, unto the days of David; who found favour before God, and desired to find a tabernacle for the God of Jacob.

But Solomon built him an house. Howbeit the most High dwelleth not in temples made with hands; as saith the prophet,

Heaven is my throne, And earth is my footstool: What house will ye build me? saith the Lord: Or what is the place of my rest? Hath not my hand made all these things?

And here he goes.

Ye stiffnecked and uncircumcised in heart and ears, ye do always resist the Holy Ghost: as your fathers did, so do ye. Which of the prophets have not your fathers persecuted?

Jesus said the same.

and they have slain them which shewed before of the coming of the Just One; of whom ye have been now the betrayers and murderers: who have received the law by the disposition of angels, and have not kept it.

When they heard these things, they were cut to the heart, and they gnashed on him with their teeth.

They started biting him. These are grown people, supposedly civilized. But when the truth came and God called them for what they were stiff-necked, stiff-necked and also rebellious and told them what they were guilty of, persecuting the just one, they couldn't take the truth. Doesn't that sound familiar today?

They have killed those that stand up and tell the truth. They'll call them devils. But Jesus said that they have called the master of the house Beelzebub. How much more they of his household. Amen. Because we dare declare the truth. Even as Stephen did. Stephen is getting ready to go home at this point.

And he's declaring the full truth. He says,

But he being full of the Holy Ghost,

this is when they started biting him,

looked up stedfastly into heaven, and saw the glory of God, and Jesus standing on the right hand of God, and said, Behold, I see the heavens opened, and the Son of man standing on the right hand of God.

Jesus was no longer seated at the right hand of God. He is standing up, giving Stephen a standing ovation because Stephen is about to come home. Preaching the gospel, preaching the truth. He preached from Moses, being a lad, a babe in Egypt to Moses, declaring the truth and giving the 10 commandments to the children of Israel.

And he goes on down to preach about the prophets prophesying of the coming of the just one. God raising up a prophet, just like Moses. But Moses was part of the house.

Jesus was over the house and still is. So he's greater than a prophet Moses, according to Hebrews. Hallelujah.

And said,

> *Behold, I see the heavens opened, and the Son of man standing on the right hand of God. Then they cried out with a loud voice, and stopped their ears,*

Don't want to hear.

> *and ran upon him with one accord, and cast him out of the city, and stoned him: and the witnesses laid down their clothes at a young man's feet, whose name was Saul.*

Who is now called Paul, we know him as Paul. The one that received the great revelations of Jesus Christ later.

> *And they stoned Stephen, calling upon God.*

Stephen calling upon God and saying,

> *Lord Jesus, receive my spirit. And he kneeled down and cried with a loud voice, lay not this sin to their charge. And when he had said this, he fell asleep.*

He went home to be with Jesus. Hallelujah. My God, my God, this Jesus is coming again. And I want to continue this subject, the day of the Lord. I'm just breaking ground here, being led by the Holy Spirit to give you to know as we continue in the word of God, who Jesus is and who he shall be when he comes again to this earth the second time. But it is time for you to call on the name of the Lord.

If you're going to be caught up in the rapture, it doesn't matter who you say you are. It's time to call on the name of the Lord that you might be saved and your sins washed away with his blood in his name. Amen.

The Earth Shall Be Shaken

Praise the Lord, everyone. We thank God for the opportunity to come to you again in the precious and powerful name of Jesus Christ, the only name that is to be reverenced in this day or any other day. The name of the Lord is a strong tower the righteous runneth into it and is safe. That's how powerful the name of the Lord Jesus truly is. And we thank God that we bear his name.

I know you in Radio Land that truly belongs to the Lord Jesus Christ and to the Father. Our God can truly say, God is to be praised and his name is to be glorified for his name is above every name. And we all will say, hallelujah, in that day, right along with the scriptures, that every knee shall bow and every tongue will confess, shall confess that Jesus Christ is Lord indeed.

We're on the topic of the day of the Lord, that great and mighty day when the Lord shall come, shall return to the earth the second time. And to make it very clear to you that have been listening to our messages these last three Sundays, including today, the Lord has been given us to know that when he comes back to this earth the second time, he is coming for war. He's coming to declare war on those that have declared war on his people, Israel, the Israelites, Israelis as we know today.

That country called Israel was given to the children of God, to the children, the seed of Abraham, generations ago, ages ago. And God has talked about his people and the land of Israel ever since. He promised Abraham that everywhere his foot would tread, he would give him that land because of Abraham's obedience in believing God when he spoke.

There is a reward to everyone that believes God when he speaks. And that's what God is requiring of every person under the sun. Believe God, believe his word, believe those that are reporting his word.

Those that are reporting God's word will never speak their own words. They will speak what thus said the Lord. That has always been and always will be until the Lord comes again. Praise his holy name.

Let us pray. We give thanks to you, Father God, in Jesus' name. And boldly we come to the throne of grace that we might obtain your mercy and find grace to help us in the time of need. Lord, sanctify our ears today. Touch our ears. Touch our hearts. Touch our eyes that we might hear and see and receive that engrafted word and cause us to stand in the power of your word, to stand in the power of your name. And we must glorify your name, enable us to do just that, to glorify the name of the Lord.

For you are our strong and mighty tower. You are the highest Lord and we give glory unto you. You are our refuge and our strength in any trouble, in any time of trouble. And when the going is good, you're still our high tower. You're still our strength and our divine refuge. My Father, I ask that your word will penetrate every heart, including mine this day.

That O God, you will accomplish that that you send your word to perform. We know that it shall not return unto your void and let it do its proper work this day. For thy word is power. Thy word is meat indeed. Glory to God. Help us to embrace thy word in the glorious name of thy son, Jesus.

And those that are out of the ark of safety, out from under the blood of Jesus Christ, we pray that the spirit of God will draw them unto Jesus. Draw, Father. No man can come to you except you draw them. And we're asking for salvation of the souls of men, women, boys and girls. Glory to God in the highest. Let thy word go forth to strengthen Zion, even us that are in Zion this day.

And those that are watching and listening, Father, draw them into the ark of safety by thy divine spirit, we pray. And let the enemy be bound on every side. Every foul, wicked one that would come to oppose the word of God, bring down in Jesus' authoritative name.

Hallelujah. And let the word of God go forth freely in the power and demonstration of the Holy Ghost by reviving the souls of your people, reviving and replenishing the work of your people. Praise God. Do your mighty work in us all and help us to look forward to these mighty events with joy and glad expectations. In thy name, Jesus, we pray, amen and amen.

According to the word of God, as we read from the book of Acts chapter 7 in its fullness in the last broadcast, I'll read verse 37 and verse 38 of Acts 7 to let you know where we are.

This is that Moses, which said unto the children of Israel, A prophet shall the Lord your God raise up unto you of your brethren, like unto me; him shall ye hear. This is he, that was in the church in the wilderness with the angel which spake to him in the mount Sina, and with our fathers: who received the lively oracles to give unto us.

And we thank God for the church that was in the wilderness. We thank God also for the Lord God bringing the church that was in the wilderness, gathering them to hear the word of the Lord. And Moses prophesied of the Messiah, of the Lord Jesus Christ, that the Lord God would raise up a prophet like unto Moses.

But in the book of Hebrews, we see that Jesus Christ is Lord over the house, even Moses. And remember when Jesus was caught up in the Mount of Transfiguration, there stood Moses and Elijah, Elijah conferring with Jesus Christ concerning the events that were to take place, proving that he is Lord even over all the prophets of the Old Testament. Jesus said of himself, before Abraham was, I am.

They wanted to kill him for that. Praise God, because they said he was, he was a blasphemous person to speak things. And he was only a 30 some years old and Abraham had long died. He had long gone on to his reward, but people not being able to discern nor being able to hear the word of the Lord, they will speak evil of the dignities of the most high God, like we hear and see today, speaking evil of those things that they understand not to their own destruction. That is not good, it is not wise.

But concerning the day of the Lord, this is what this text is all about. The day of the Lord. This is not the time when Jesus will come on a cloud and hover there for a moment or so together, the saints together, his bride unto himself out of the world from all the four corners of the world, for those that have made themselves ready, according to the book of

Revelation, the bride hath made herself ready. She went after God with all her heart and all her soul, with all her might and with all her love and with all her strength and made herself ready to meet the Lord in the air. Amen.

That event we're all looking forward unto, it shall surely come to pass quickly. And very soon, we do know, but he will not come to the earth. He will be on a cloud to catch us up, to meet him and bring us home, to present us to the father, to present his bride to the father.

But one day, Jesus is going to come back to this earth after the bride has been in his presence for seven years in glory in heaven, gathered there with all the saints that have made themselves ready to meet him and to be with him forevermore. Jesus will come again when the bride is taken out. There should be great tribulation upon the face of this earth and there should be great bondage and the evil beast will show himself, the false prophet will show himself, the antichrist spirit will show himself.

It will be a lot of woes in this earth and it's all written down in the book of life. It's written down in this gospel and in the book of Revelation. These things are written that we might read and hear and fear God and obey him.

Hallelujah. But many will read, but they will not obey God because many do not believe the report that is given. But I'm here to tell you, I am one that believe all the word of God, rightly divided.

Jesus is coming to this earth to declare war on the enemies of God that will be trying to overtake Israel. We see Israel in all the newspapers all over the world that has newspapers today. Israel, the timetable of God, for nationalities all around this globe called the earth to look at and gaze at, to let us see where we stand as individuals in the eyes of God.

And as we look and we see the things that are taking place and things according to the scriptures that are yet to take place over in Israel, we know that our redemption draws nigh. In the book of Acts, as I just read, the Lord moved upon Stephen, the martyr of the church of Jesus Christ, to talk to his people, to tell his people, the Israelites, who Jesus really is. And he took them back in history from Abraham all the way up until his appointed time.

And he spoke to them history and they heard and they became enraged because their heart had no faith and they knew not God that visited them in sending his son, the Messiah, Jesus Christ. They rejected him. And one day, Israel, all Israel will acknowledge that Jesus Christ is truly indeed the Messiah as a whole, only a little sprinkling here and a little sprinkling there upon the Israelites as they come in into the knowledge of the truth.

And one day, that great and mighty day, when nations of the world will try to overtake Israel, will try to eliminate Israel altogether. This is what God is saying, found in the book of Ezekiel. Chapter 39 of the book of Ezekiel, I'll begin at 38. Gog is to invade, restore Palestine in the last days.

Verse 8,

> *After many days thou shalt be visited: in the latter years thou shalt come into the land that is brought back from the sword, and is gathered out of many people, against the mountains of Israel, which have been always waste: but it is brought forth out of the*

*nations, and they shall dwell safely all of
them. Thou shalt ascend and come like a storm,*

He's talking about the enemies of God. I'm in Ezekiel 38, verse 9.

*Thou shalt ascend and come like a storm, thou shalt
be like a cloud to cover the land, thou, and all thy
bands, and many people with thee.*

*Thus saith the Lord GOD; It shall also come to
pass, that at the same time shall things come into
thy mind, and thou shalt think an evil thought: and
thou shalt say, I will go up to the land of unwalled
villages;*

*I will go to them that are at rest, that dwell safely,
all of them dwelling without walls, and having
neither bars nor gates, to take a spoil, and to take a
prey; to turn thine hand upon the desolate
places that are now inhabited, and upon the
people that are gathered out of the nations, which
have gotten cattle and goods, that dwell in the midst
of the land.*

God is saying, even though my people are there, I brought them back out of nations, different nations of the earth. I brought them back to the land that I have promised their forefathers.

And I am keeping my promise that I gave to Abraham. Abraham set his foot in the land of Canaan and the Lord God promised Abraham that his seed would dwell there and forever… This is forever.

No one has no right to take anything from that that God has given. But because of covetousness, because of jealousy, because of pride, because of prejudice, many have fought and won many battles over the children of men. This is the heart of man, this is how man thinks. I'll invade your territory, and I will take it over completely. I won't ask you for it, I'll take it. This is the heart of man, when that heart is not yielded to God.

But the Lord says in verse 14,

> *Therefore, son of man, prophesy and say unto Gog, Thus saith the Lord GOD; In that day when my people of Israel dwelleth safely, shalt thou not know it?*

> *And thou shalt come from thy place out of the north parts, thou, and many people with thee, all of them riding upon horses, a great company, and a mighty army: and thou shalt come up against my people of Israel, as a cloud to cover the land; it shall be in the latter days, and I will bring thee against my land*

The Lord said, I will bring thee against my land

> *that the heathen may know me when I shall be sanctified in thee, O God, before their eyes.*

Remember Egypt? Remember how Pharaoh stood against Moses when God led Moses in to bring his people out? God allowed that king's heart to be hardened that God may show forth the mighty power of deliverance. God is a God of deliverance, and he knows the heart of man.

He knows who will humble themselves and submit to God's authority. And God also knows those who will not humble themselves, but will fight against God. We'll see they are like their father, the devil. Remember when Lucifer was in heaven, he said, I will ascend before the throne of God as he has that same heart today in many people worldwide.

 But God is the authority. God almighty, the great I am Jehovah Jireh is his name. His name is also called Jah. Hallelujah. He is the authority.

He is the everlasting Creator. He is the everlasting Father. He is the everlasting Almighty God.

And God will never allow the devil nor man to have the last say nor the last fight. God is going to fight. And when He fights, everything is going down that is not of God. The Lord said, I'm going to read 17 again,

> *Thus saith the Lord GOD; Art thou he of whom I have spoken in old time by my servants the prophets of Israel, which prophesied in those days many years that I would bring thee against them?*

And if you look here is Ezekiel, Isaiah, Zechariah, Moses, the books of Moses, you name it. It is written there in Revelation. It is written there what God said he will do. And they were faithful to write these things down. Now, perhaps there were nonbelievers and mockers of their day like we have in our day. And when they did not see these things come to pass, they said, oh, they're crazy, don't believe them.

But God will never allow his word to go out and return to him void to prove that he knows the end from the beginning. He moves upon his servants to speak the word of God, no matter how long it takes.

Many think we're Christians today that are looking for the return of the Lord to come and receive us unto himself as He comes on the cloud and the power of God raises us up from this world. They think we are crazy but bless the Lord, we're enclosed in the mind of Christ.

We have the mind of Christ, and the Lord tells us to look for his coming. He said, the things that we see happening now, when we see these things come to pass, look up for your redemption draweth nigh.

And we're looking up, we're looking around us and we are not fools and blind. We see what's happening. We see the great persecutions against the true children of God, but we are rejoicing because we know our time is short here on this earth.

Israel will have to go through this great tribulation period in order to get her eyes open to realize that Jesus came the first time and they rejected him. When he comes the second time to deliver them from Gog and Magog and all the nations of the earth that have joined with Gog and Magog to fight the Israelis, the Israelites, they are going to realize when Jesus put all wars down, they're going to know and recognize that Jesus Christ is the Messiah indeed. But before we go there, time does not permit us today.

I want to continue to read verse 19 of Ezekiel 38,

> *For in my jealousy and in the fire of my wrath have I spoken, Surely in that day there shall be a great shaking in the land of Israel; so that the fishes of the sea, and the fowls of the heaven, and the beasts of the field, and all creeping things that creep upon the earth, and all the men that are upon the face of the earth, shall shake at my presence.*

This is God Almighty. How the hearts of people shake and fear when we hear a great thundering in the heavens, the voice of God, we are told from the word of God.

How much more when there'll be thunderings and thunderings, the voice of God, like many waters moving. Glory be to God. And God shaking the earth itself, not just in Israel, but shaking the world itself and showing them who is the greatest.

He's waited and suffered a long time for men to come to their senses and repent of their sins. And because they refuse and became enemies in their hearts willfully against the Almighty, the Lord said there shall be a great shaking, a great shaking. Let me read verse 20 again,

> *So that the fishes of the sea, and the fowls of the heaven, and the beasts of the field, and all creeping things that creep upon the earth, and all the men that are upon the face of the earth, shall shake at my presence, and the mountains shall be thrown down, and the steep places shall fall, and every wall shall fall to the ground. And I will call for a sword against him throughout all my mountains, saith the Lord GOD: every man's sword shall be against his brother. And I will plead against him with pestilence and with blood; and I will rain upon him, and upon his bands, and upon the many people that are with him, an overflowing rain, and great hailstones, fire, and brimstone.*

Look at the things that we see today, earthquakes and fire, even in our own nation. You see the horribleness of it all...It's horrible. You see what's happening and people running for their lives, having to leave what they have built and worked a long time for to save their own lives. That's nothing compared to the wrath of God that is to come... That is to come.

He says,

> Thus will I magnify myself, and sanctify myself; and I will be known in the eyes of many nations, and they shall know that I am the LORD.

Man is going to shake. There's a lot of shaking going on, but God hasn't started. When God starts shaking, God's not going to let up until he has been appeased. God loves the souls of all mankind everywhere, but God hates the sins and the abominations that man is committing. He hates idolatry. God hates what man is doing to one another.

Jesus came to show us the way to the father. Jesus came speaking the words of life to every living creature, every living human being under the sun and only a few are listening.

Comparing to the majority of the world, billions of the world, the gospel is going out by radio, by satellite, you name it. Whatever means God has, he is using for the glory of God to cause the people to hear the truth and be made free and many are listening, but not turning to this most high God.

I'm here to tell you this word is written for a purpose and we have to give it for a purpose. God moves by design, plans and purposes and his word shall come to pass. Many people in that day will run to seek to hide. They'll run to the rocks to seek to hide from the presence of God Almighty, but they cannot stand.

The rocks will cry out, no hiding place. I'll show you from continuing reading in the book of prophecies, Ezekiel and revelation in different places of the book, what God will be like in that day and he will not be appeased at all until His will has been accomplished upon his enemies. But know that God loves Israel and we will do wise ourselves to pray for Israel in Jesus name. God be with you. Amen and amen.

King Jesus Makes War

Praise God from whom all blessings flow. God is to be glorified in all that we say and all that we do. And I do thank God and praise him for the privilege that he has bestowed upon me to speak the Word of God concerning the last day. I'm reading from the Word of God in Ezekiel 39, chapter 39. You that have your Bibles, please turn with me there.

We're talking about the last day, that great and mighty day of the Lord. That day when the Lord Jesus Christ will come back to the earth to declare war on the nations of the world, because they have failed to give him honor and glory. And they have warred against God's apple, the apple of God's eye, Israel. Israel, the land that God gave his people, the Israelites of old.

The Lord gave it. The Lord owns the world. The world is the Lord's, the earth is the Lord's and the fullness thereof. God made it by speaking the world into existence. Not only this world, God has made other worlds. It is plural.

God made the worlds. He spoke them into existence and ever since the worlds were made, man, God made to inhabit the earth and man has tried to explore and has been exploring the things that God has created ever since. And that's all right, because God is to be glorified.

God is to be magnified in the eyes of man. But God is God and man is man. And we are, we that are born again are the children of the Most High God, and our hearts are where God is. We think on heaven. We think on the manifestation of God and his power, not only in heaven, but in earth.

It's our hope and our comfort because we know that we are in a world that is not only inhabited by man, but it's also overrun by demonic activity. No, I don't glory in the works of the devil. I despise him.

And I'm reminded of Jesus Christ when he came teaching and speaking what the Father, the words that the Father put in his heart to bring forth unto the children of men. He also talked about hell, giving us to know that there is an awful place that is prepared for the devil and his angels, the ones that warred and rose up against God, their creator in heaven, God has cast down, bound with everlasting chains of darkness.

And they're the ones that go around raising havoc on the earth and the air, doing ugly and wicked things to destroy the life that God has given unto men and not only unto men, but to destroy the earth that God has made for us to inhabit.

So Jesus, when he comes again, the second time to this earth, he is not coming as the savior of all mankind. He is coming back as a mighty warrior, as the captain of every soldier that will be coming back with him to put down all demonic activity.

And Satan himself will be bound a thousand years, the angel of God from on high will have a chain in his hand and he just one angel of the Lord will bind Satan for a thousand years. Hallelujah. It shall happen.

It is going to happen whether we believe it or not, but I'm one that believe, I believe the word of God. I believe everything that is proceeded out of the mouth of God. I believe I am wise enough to believe God and tremble at his word that I might be ready when Jesus comes to take his bride out of this world before all this great tribulation comes upon this world.

We are looking and listening to leaders of the world preparing for one world government. They're actually preparing for the Antichrist spirit to take over the world. And there is going to be a suffering in this world, great persecution like the world has never known or heard of.

It has never been recorded in the history of man what is about to take place once the bride of Christ has been taken out of this world and many will lose their lives eternally so because they have not known God.

And when the beast shows himself, he's not going to reveal himself immediately when the bride of Christ is taken out of here, out of this world to be with the Father and with the son and all the saints in glory. We are going to escape the damnations and the diabolical things that are coming upon the face of this earth invented by Satan himself and by that false prophet and by that diabolical beast that is to show themselves later, but not at first.

They will use great deception. This is why we see great activity of deceit in the world today amongst the rulers of the world. Great deceit. No one truly speaking the truth one to another. No man even valiant for the truth because Satan is setting up his kingdom in the hearts of the rulers of this world and we see it happening. We see hearts that are full of murder, full of destruction, full of meanness with no desire to see souls saved and no mercy in the heart whatsoever.

We look at road rage today and we wonder what's going on. It's easy to understand. Satan is preparing the hearts of men to destroy one another, to despise one another. See to destroy you have to despise, you have to hate. God is love. He's just the opposite of what I have just spoken.

God is love and he's merciful, He's patient, He's long suffering and every person under the sun, if they honestly confess the truth, will say that God has been merciful to us.

He's been long suffering. He's been patient and we, mankind, has put God through much agony and yet his hands are outstretched to bring deliverance even now. But one day the mercy of God will close.

God is coming to declare war on all the kingdoms of this world on the behalf of Israel and on the behalf of God himself. Because God ages ago made a covenant with Abraham, his friend, and God is keeping that promise. Abraham is resting in the bosom of God today, but God is keeping his promise. In the book of Ezekiel chapter 39, let us read.

Before we start reading, let's pray...

Father God, before the throne of grace, we come in Jesus' mighty name, knowing that we have access to your throne and we are heard by you every time we approach You because you are full of grace and truth. And you desire that we make known our request to you because you're ready to answer.

You're God that answers prayer. You put it in our hearts by your spirit. You give us utterance before you. And this day we are depending upon the Holy Spirit to give us utterance before the throne of God in the precious and wonderful name of thy son, Jesus. Thank you, Father, for thy word that you have established in the earth. And you said your word shall never return unto you void.

What you have sent it out to do, what you have spoken into existence, it shall be performed. And we thank you for it. And Lord, there'll be many that have not known or heard the things that you're using me to speak and to read from your word, but you have ordained this time that this handmaiden of yours will speak your truth in the last day that the Lord will come and bring down all abominations and set Your kingdom to rule and reign over the face of this world.

And you shall govern every nation under the sun. Hallelujah. No democracy, but theocracy. Oh God, you will do your work. You will perform your will and you will rule with the rod of iron. Help us to hear your word today.

Help us, Lord, to speak your word through the unction of the Holy Spirit. We lean upon you, Holy Ghost. Thy will be done, Father. Thy word be heard. You said the humble shall hear thereof and be glad. Help us to humble ourselves before your mighty hand that you may exalt us over these things that are coming on the face of this earth. In Jesus' name we pray.

Ezekiel 39,

> *Therefore, thou son of man, prophesy against Gog, and say, Thus saith the Lord GOD; Behold, I am against thee, O Gog, the chief prince of Meshech and Tubal: and I will turn thee back, and leave but the sixth part of thee, and will cause thee*

> *to come up from the north parts, and will bring thee upon the mountains of Israel*

I'm retracking, but it's important that I do so.

> *Thou shalt fall upon the mountains of Israel, thou, and all thy bands, and the people that is with thee: I will give thee unto the ravenous birds of every sort, and to the beasts of the field to be devoured.*

He's talking to Gog, and Magog, those that are making war, those that are starting war against the Israelites, against the nation Israel, the small little nation called Israel.

> *Thou shalt fall upon the open field: for I have spoken it, saith the Lord GOD. And I will send a fire on Magog, and among them that dwell carelessly in the isles: and they shall know that I am the LORD.*

This is why it's important for us not to be careless when God speaks, and not to be idle when God speaks, because God does not overlook idleness. He does not overlook carelessness. We're to care about what God says, and we're to care about the things that God has created.

He said,

> *I will send a fire, on Magog, and among them that dwell carelessly in the aisles, and they shall know that I am the Lord. So will I make my holy name known in the midst of my people Israel.*

Listen to what he is saying,

> *and I will not let them pollute my holy name any more.*

Man has freely spoken his own mind and spoken the evils of his heart without fear against the holy God of Israel, but God said no more in that day.

> *And I will not let them pollute my holy name any more, and the heathen shall know that I am the Lord, the Holy One of Israel.*

They shall know that I am the Lord, the Holy One of Israel. He's coming back to Israel.

> *Behold, it is come, and it is done, saith the Lord GOD; this is the day whereof I have spoken.*

Now he's speaking in the future tense as in the present tense. Behold, it is done. Do you know when God speaks something, it can be years ahead, but in God's eyes, it is already done. It is already accomplished. That's how great he is. That's how mighty he is and no one can stop him. There is no flood, there is no fire, there is no army in any nation, no satellite, no spy team of any sort that can stop God. It's all written here, it's in the book.

I appeal to the leaders of the nations in which my voice is being heard as I minister the word of God. I appeal unto you by the grace of the Lord God Almighty, and in the name of his son, Jesus, that you hear the word of God and humble yourselves and do his will.

There are going to be kings that will bring their glory into the kingdom of God. I pray that you will be one of them. Because if you declare in your heart that you will not believe God and you blaspheme that holy name by which we are called, God will pour out his wrath against you.

It's pending. This is why God has put this upon my heart. You that will fear him as you hear his word, God is seeking to save your soul, to bring you into safety. His name is safety. If you come unto him in the name of his son, Jesus, the Lord will preserve your life. All that are not preserved, God's wrath will be poured upon.

Let me read verse seven again.

> *So will I make my holy name known in the midst of my people Israel; and I will not let them pollute my holy name any more: and the heathen shall know that I am the LORD, the Holy One in Israel.*

You will know beyond any doubt the Holy One in Israel.

> *Behold, it is come, and it is done, saith the Lord GOD; this is the day whereof I have spoken.*

He's speaking as if it's already done, and it will be.

> *And they that dwell in the cities of Israel shall go forth, and shall set on fire and burn the weapons, both the shields and the bucklers, the bows and the arrows, and the handstaves, and the spears, and they shall burn them with fire seven years:*

Seven years they will be burning the weapons that others have brought up to destroy Israel. Can you think of that in the fullness? Seven years it's going to take the Israelis to burn the weapons that was brought up by other nations to destroy that one little country,

> *so that they shall take no wood out of the field, neither cut down any out of the forests; for they shall burn the weapons with fire: and they shall spoil those that spoiled them, and rob those that robbed them, saith the Lord GOD.*

*And it shall come to pass in that day, that I will give
unto Gog a place there of graves in Israel, the
valley of the passengers on the east of the sea: and
it shall stop the noses of the passengers: and there
shall they bury Gog and all his multitude: and they
shall call it The valley of Hamon-gog.*

*And seven months shall the house of Israel be
burying of them, that they may cleanse the land*

There's going to be a great battle fought in the valley of
Megiddo.

*Yea, all the people of the land shall bury them; and
it shall be to them a renown the day that I shall be
glorified, saith the Lord GOD.*

Everyone is going to know who God is. They're going to
know that this is the one that created the heavens and the
earth. God is going to put down every nation that has risen
up against Israel,

*And they shall sever out men of continual
employment, passing through the land to bury with
the passengers those that remain upon the face of
the earth,*

In other words, those that have not been buried. They're
going to spend all of that time, all of those months, burying
those that have been slaughtered by the Lord speaking His
word.

*To cleanse it after the end of seven months shall
they search.*

They're going to search for dead bodies.

*And the passengers that pass through the land,
when any seeth a man's bone, then shall he set up a
sign by it, till the buriers have buried it in the valley
of Hamon-gog. And also the name of the city shall
be Hamonah. Thus shall they cleanse the land.*

It's going to happen. There's going to be a great slaughter, and the Lord, the Lord Jesus Christ will be the leader thereof. Hallelujah. It's time to get on the Lord's side.

This Christ in whom we celebrate at Christmas as the babe that was born in Bethlehem is no longer a babe. In this day, he will no longer be the savior of the world. He is going to be the mighty warrior from on high.

He is going to open the heavens and ride out of heaven on a white horse with his vesture dipped in blood. And on His thigh shall be named the King of Kings, the Lord of Lords and the King of Kings. Hallelujah.

Jesus Christ is coming as the mighty warrior, not to save the sinner from their sins, but to destroy the sinners from meddling with his affairs. God the Father is going to send his son as the captain of this great army. And there are going to be white horses riding behind Jesus's white horse out of the heavens coming to declare war on the face of this earth because of the madness of Satan and the leaders of the world as they gather together to eliminate Israel.

It won't happen. Hallelujah. God has spoken it and He said it is done!

It is done. It's time to get on the Lord's side. You Christians that have been so faint hearted, refusing to stand up in Christ Jesus and be accounted as a soldier of Jesus Christ.

It's time to get on the Lord's side. It's time to bear His name. And yes, the reproach that comes against his name.

It's time to stand, make a firm stand in the Lord. It's time to come out of the valid decision and make Jesus Christ your trust. He'll be your friend in that day.

If you don't allow him to be your friend now. We don't allow him to be your savior and your Lord now. He's going to rule in that day.

Where will you be? Where will you be? He's not playing.

Too long, mankind has taken the mercies of God for granted and trampled his mercies on the feet. And it's been presumptuous concerning his love. Stop that nonsense. No more time for that nonsense.

It's time to take God at his word and tremble and fear God. And make yourself ready to meet Jesus because he's coming for his bride before all of this takes place. Hallelujah.

The great tribulation period is coming, but the bride of Christ will be taken out of here and all hell's going to break loose on the face of this earth, as I said at the beginning, deceit will be the rule of the day. Deception on every side.

Diabolical forces of witchcrafts and great sorceries. That is how the prophet, that a false prophet will rule. It will be through great sorceries, deceiving the people, blinding their minds, hardening their hearts.

It'll be a great day when Jesus comes to put down the works of Satan, he's going to be bound, he will be bound.

The Lord says,

> *And, thou son of man, thus saith the Lord GOD;*
> *Speak unto every feathered fowl, and to every beast*
> *of the field, Assemble yourselves, and come; gather*
> *yourselves on every side to my sacrifice that I do*
> *sacrifice for you, even a great sacrifice upon the*
> *mountains of Israel, that ye may eat flesh, and drink*
> *blood.*

He is speaking to that that is created, the great fowls of the air to devour and to drink blood, those that shall be slain. He's coming as the mighty warrior from on high. It's time to get right with God. It's time to escape what's coming upon the face of this earth. Because in that day, no one will have a chance to get right.

When Jesus comes to set his feet on Mount Olives, even a mountain will split in two. That's how powerful Jesus is. He's Lord of heaven and earth.

And that will be only the beginning of the wrath of God displayed in that day. It's coming upon those that despise God and that has made a covenant with the devil, that has made pledges with their lives and stayed on the devil's side. They're going down…They're going down.

And it's time to think soberly. It is time to make Jesus Christ your Lord, your Savior, and your friend now before it's eternally too late. God is not playing with man. God is speaking his word. The prophecies of God from the beginning are beginning to come to pass in these days in which we are living.

The stage has been set. Get right with God. Amen.

Get Ready to Meet Him

We give honor to the Most High God and to Jesus Christ, our Lord, and our soon coming King. Hallelujah. Let us pray.

Dear Father, before the throne of grace, we come boldly in the name of Thy Son, Jesus. We thank you for the word of life. We thank you for the gospel of Jesus Christ.

We thank you, Lord, for those that are carrying the gospel of Jesus Christ, faithfully proclaiming thy word, uttered by the Holy Spirit, unctioned by the Holy Spirit and power. Unto you, Lord, we give this service. Cause your mighty word to be heard. Cause our ears to be sanctified, our hearts to be sanctified, our eyes to be sanctified and empowered by the Holy Spirit, that our hearts might receive that engrafted word. And we may know where we are today, according to the calendar of the Most High God. Thy kingdom come, thy will be done in the greatness of your power.

Show forth thy word this day, even to the unbelievers in heart, that all men everywhere might be warned and might know that you are the Christ indeed. Save the souls, Lord, as thy word goes forth. Strengthen those in Zion that belongs to you. Strengthen, Lord God. Praise your holy name. Cause us to be sober before you.

And those that are outside of the ark of safety, outside of the blood of Jesus, draw by your spirit this day. Call men and women, boys and girls, to hear your voice and prepare for your coming. Watch over your word. Cause it to do what you have sent it to do. Work miracles in each heart that will believe you. Change hearts, change minds, bring into your captivity.

Break the bands of wickedness asunder. Cut the cords of wickedness asunder and let the oppressed go free. Let the sick and afflicted in heart and soul and body be liberated this day by the power of thy son's name, Jesus.

In your name, Lord, do a mighty work this day and send your word and heal this day. And let the wicked be warned. You're God almighty.

Hallelujah. In Jesus name, let the enemy be bound and put down. And let the word of God go forth richly in the authority of Jesus's name. Amen and amen.

We're speaking and have been for several weeks now concerning the day of the Lord. There is a great and mighty day coming that belongs to God alone. He will prove who he is. He shall show forth his glory and his might and power. Yes, his military power. Hallelujah.

There's no military power like the power of Jesus Christ. We see the military in different nations of the earth showing forth their might and their strength, but there is no might and no strength that can compare or measure up to the strength of the almighty God.

And one day, the day of the Lord that shall come, God will exercise his power and his might before all the world. Great showmanship? No… Authority, authority!

He's the authority over all the world. He is the authority. No man can know any authority like Jesus Christ.

I want to read from the 14th chapter of Zechariah. We'll begin there concerning the subject of the day of the Lord. Zechariah writes,

> *Behold, the day of the LORD cometh, and thy spoil shall be divided in the midst of thee. For I will gather all nations against Jerusalem to battle;*

You see the authority of Christ. He shall gather all nations. Now, all nations may think that they are coming for a reason, and they may think that it's their thoughts and their hearts to eliminate the Israelites altogether and take over the land of Israel.

But the Lord said, I will gather all nations against Jerusalem to battle, not to overthrow Jerusalem or Israel, but to overthrow the nations in Israel.

> *I will gather all nations against Jerusalem to battle; and the city shall be taken, and the houses rifled, and the women ravished; and half of the city shall go forth into captivity, and the residue of the people shall not be cut off from the city. Then shall the LORD go forth, and fight against those nations, as when he fought in the day of battle.*

The Lord's going to gather them that they might show forth the wickedness and the evilness and the meanness and the murder that's in their hearts and the covetousness and the greed. The Lord God is going to gather them against his beloved Israel. And those that will be ravished and those that will be overtaken will be those that will not accept Jesus Christ as Lord and Savior.

People are trying to do everything to respect one another's religion. Their faith, their religion, but there's only one Lord, one faith, and one baptism. This is the truth, and every man is going to acknowledge the truth, if not now, later on, that they will see for themselves.

The wisest thing to do is to believe on the Lord Jesus Christ and accept him as Lord Messiah, Yeshua, the Savior of all men. In verse 4, here's how the Lord is going to come back the second time,

> *And his feet shall stand in that day upon the mount of Olives, which is before Jerusalem on the east, and the mount of Olives shall cleave in the midst thereof toward the east and toward the west, and there shall be a very great valley; and half of the mountain shall remove toward the north, and half of it toward the south.*

God's going to split the mountain when his powerful feet lands on Mount Olive. Many of you have been to Israel on tours, myself included. And I've stood on Mount Olive, and I've looked over the city of Jerusalem. I've seen the old part of Jerusalem and all the surrounding buildings and the newest part. It's a wonder to behold.

Jesus, when he comes back to the earth the second time, he is coming to Mount Olive. And he's going to have such power even in his feet that the mountain will actually split in two, and it describes how the mountain will split.

And in verse five he said,

> And ye shall flee *to* the valley of the mountains; for the valley of the mountains shall reach unto Azal: yea, ye shall flee, like as ye fled from before the

earthquake in the days of Uzziah king of Judah: and the LORD my God shall come, *and* all the saints with thee

All the saints are coming with the Lord God Almighty. His name is Jesus Christ. Hallelujah. Now, how in the world will all the saints be coming with him? Because when Jesus comes to rapture the church, the bride of Jesus Christ, those that are watching and looking for his return to be caught up to escape the tribulation period, that will last seven years, and the latter half, the three and a half last years of the great tribulation period will be with great suffering, great suffering like never before on the history of man.

But the church of Jesus, the bride of Christ, as we read in Revelations, how the bride of Christ has made herself ready. We that are washed in the blood and not just singing little praise songs, but living holy, righteous and dedicated, consecrated unto the Lord, looking at the things that are happening on the face of this earth and drawing even closer to Jesus Christ, the bridegroom. We have oil in our vessels, our lamps are trimmed, and we're looking and we're listening for the trumpet sound because he's coming back to bring his bride out of this hellish world.

This world is full of hell itself. Hell from beneath is oozing out demons day by day and overtaking the children of men because of their rebellion against the almighty God and their rejection against the love gift of God. That rejection is causing men and women, boys and girls, to be separated from this God of love and this God of mercy and this God of forgiveness.

The nature of God is to forgive, to restore, to make whole. And man, because of his desire to do evil, and he hates the goodness of God, he hates the light of righteousness. They choose to do evil and abide in darkness. And because of this, their heart is more cold than ever. Life means nothing to many out there. Thievery, robbery, murder, you name it…

It's out there and it's getting gross. The wickedness of man is becoming more gross day by day, hour by hour. And they will not be ready to meet Jesus when he comes for his bride. The carnal-minded Christian won't be ready. The lukewarm-hearted Christian will not be ready. Remember what Jesus said in the book of Revelation? I would that you be hot or cold, but because you're lukewarm, I shall spew you out of my mouth, I'll just spit you out. That's what Jesus said. The King of glory, as we know him so merciful and gracious today.

Let's see all of God, not just the part we want to see. Let's see all of God as the Holy Spirit will reveal him. That's the ministry of the Holy Spirit. The Holy Ghost is to reveal the Lord Jesus Christ to the believers, and we see him. Hallelujah.

I thank God for this message that he is putting upon my heart and many other ministers' hearts to proclaim this last day message. No one will be able to tell the Lord Jesus Christ or God the Father. I didn't know, I didn't understand.

You never told me. All you've got to do is take time to listen because the Spirit of God is dealing with the consciousness of man daily, daily!

He is convicting and he's pricking the hearts of mankind to stop sinning and turn to the Lord God that made you, and many won't hear. There's a day coming, it's called the day of the Lord. Hallelujah.

In verse 6,

> *And it shall come to pass in that day, that the light shall not be clear, nor dark: but it shall be one day which shall be known to the LORD, not day, nor night: but it shall come to pass, that at evening time it shall be light.*

> *And it shall be in that day, that living waters shall go out from Jerusalem; half of them toward the former sea, and half of them toward the hinder sea: in summer and in winter shall it be. And the LORD shall be king over all the earth:*

The Lord Jesus Christ.

> *in that day shall there be one LORD, and his name one.*

We're trying to make him fit into our religious beliefs. It won't happen. One Lord, one faith, one baptism. It's already written down. And the Lord God said, My word shall not return unto me void. Verse 10,

> *All the land shall be turned as a plain from Geba to Rimmon south of Jerusalem: and it shall be lifted up, and inhabited in her place, from Benjamin's gate unto the place of the first gate, unto the corner gate, and from the tower of Hananeel unto the king's winepresses. And men shall dwell in it, and there shall be no more utter destruction; but Jerusalem shall be safely inhabited.*

That's when Jesus Christ puts everything in order on the face of this earth.

In chapter 13 of Zechariah, verse three,

And it shall come to pass, that when any shall yet prophesy, then his father and his mother that begat him shall say unto him, Thou shalt not live; for thou speakest lies in the name of the LORD: and his father and his mother that begat him shall thrust him through when he prophesieth.

And it shall come to pass in that day, that the prophets shall be ashamed every one of his vision, when he hath prophesied; neither shall they wear a rough garment to deceive:

See, we're living in a time of great deception. Deception on every side, political deception, religious deception, because satan is the great deceiver, his name is called deceiver. So everything that is not of God is under the deceiver's reign. He's reigning now, and he's winning souls by the hundreds and thousands and millions…the enemy, satan!

And he's got false prophets. He's raised them up to deceive the people and lie to their hearts. This is why we have the psychic things on television. We have psychics in the pulpit, false prophets, wizards, witches, everything that is false, satan has raised up like he did in Egypt when God sent Moses down to try to overthrow the plan of God. It will not work.

Jesus Christ is going to put everything down when he comes. In verse five, let me read,

but he shall say, I am no prophet, I am an husbandman; for man taught me to keep cattle from my youth.

Sound like Amos…

> *And one shall say unto him, What are these wounds in thine hands?*

This is when he comes to rule and bring peace to Israel and set his headquarters in Jerusalem. They're going to ask him, what are these wounds in thy hands?

> *Then he shall answer, those with which I was wounded in the house of my friends.*

Remember how Jesus hung on the cross? They nailed his hands to the cross. When Jesus comes to rule, after He's put down all the wickedness and destroyed the enemy, bound him a thousand years. And those wicked kings and queens and presidents and you name it. That have caused nations to come against Israel.

The Lord Jesus Christ will bring them down and they shall be destroyed. I read to you last week how it's going to take months to bury the dead. The Lord has already got vultures waiting to eat and devour the dead bodies, that he's going to destroy. The Lord Jesus Christ is coming as the warrior from on high! And no one's going to stop him because it's God's timing.

The day of the Lord! Hear me.

In verse seven,

> Awake, O sword, against my shepherd, and against the man *that is* my fellow, saith the LORD of hosts: smite the shepherd, and the sheep shall be scattered: and I will turn mine hand upon the little ones.

This is what they did, they smote Jesus Christ and his disciples ran for cover. They scattered for fear of those that had ordered the crucifixion of Jesus Christ. Zechariah prophesying under the unction of the Holy Spirit of Go, years before Christ, Jesus came as the savior of all mankind. And these are going to ask him, what are these wounds in the hand? Hallelujah. And he will answer, I was wounded in the house of my friends.

> *And it shall come to pass, that in all the land, saith the LORD, two parts therein shall be cut off and die; but the third shall be left therein.*

The inhabitants of the land of Israel, two parts or two thirds shall be cut off. Why? Because of their unbelief and their rebellion. Remember it was said long ago, we will not let this man rule over us. But he is coming not only as a man, but the King of kings and Lord of lords. And he will rule.

And if you will not let him rule, down you go. But he shall rule with a rod of iron in that great day of his thousand year reign. And he said, verse nine,

> *and I will bring the third part through the fire.*

That means great affliction, great tribulation.

> *and will refine them as silver is refined,*

This is the time of Israel's restoration back to God almighty. Hallelujah. Gentiles, we don't have long!

> *and will try them as gold is tried: they shall call on my name,*

Israel's going to call on the name of the Lord! One third of Israel will call on the name of the Lord out of a true heart.

> *and I will hear them: I will say, It is my people: and they shall say, The LORD is my God.*

They won't reject Him any longer, the proof is going to be right there in the midst of them. Hallelujah. The Lord is moving mightily by his spirit on the face of the earth. Nations are being warned to come to Jesus Christ. The invitation of salvation is being given throughout the world. Souls are being saved, marvelous things are happening in the kingdom of God here on earth.

We are spiritually and physically every believer that is born again, washed in the blood and following after the Lord Jesus Christ… We are the tabernacle of God on the earth now. We are the kingdom of God on the earth now. But there's a day coming when Jesus Christ will come and rule. And He has headquarters already planned in Jerusalem.

And this is why no one is going to overtake Jerusalem and stay there. It is the Lord's headquarters… And He will come. Praise His holy name.

And Matthew, the 24th chapter, beginning at verse 21.

> *for then shall be great tribulation, such as was not since the beginning of the world to this time, no, nor ever shall be.*

The great tribulation period we see it already getting set to manifest itself. This is why we hear people saying one world order. This is the beginning of the beast's rule, the Antichrist rule.

And saints of God, be not afraid. This is why there's actually no privacy anywhere any longer. Not only do they identify you by your social security card. We have the easy pass, they have all kinds of ways. The governments of the lands, not just America, but over all the world.

There's an increase of invading your privacy. There's no privacy act, everything is open so the Antichrist can see what each one is. That day is on us. And God is telling us to draw nigh to be ready for Jesus Christ, the bridegroom to bring us out of here…This wicked world…

That we might be able to escape this great tribulation period that is coming on the face of the earth.

What He is looking for in You

Praise the Lord. We give honor to the Most High God and to Jesus Christ, our Lord and our King, who shall be coming for the Church, the Bride of Christ, very soon. God is good and merciful and kind. As I've often said, He's good. The Lord God is good to the children of men. Everywhere, God is good and His mercies are ever upon us. His mercies are extended to the children, to the children of the earth, desiring and requiring that everyone come unto Him. Bless His holy name.

We have been ministering, been teaching concerning the second coming of the Lord Jesus Christ. Christ coming in His power, coming in His glory, coming in His wrath to put down the works of satan and the antichrist and the beast that old false prophet. This is our sixth teaching concerning the day of the Lord, that great and mighty day when Jesus comes back to the earth to let men everywhere know who God is.

We see the Lord God Almighty as a God of mercy, great mercies, and long-suffering, tender in mercy, full of love, hands outstretched to save, ever desiring to see the souls of humanity saved. John declares that God so loved the world that He gave His only begotten Son, that whosoever believeth in Him should not perish, but have everlasting life. And that's why God the Father sent the Son.

Now who would ever, who ever would believe the report given concerning Jesus Christ and accept Him as their personal Savior would be saved. That's a promise. Time is running out for many. There are yet multitudes in the valley of decision, they are not aware that time is running out before Jesus comes for the bride.

Those that have made themselves ready according to the book of Revelation, the bride hath made herself ready to receive the Lord Jesus when He comes to gather His saints or His bride up unto Him. And I want to read from the fourth chapter of 1st Thessalonians, that you might see and decide for yourself, what will it be for you? Let us pray. Thy will be done, Father, as we come before the throne of grace in the name of Thy Son Jesus, our Savior and our Lord and King.

Have preeminence over Your Word this day. Watch upon Your Word, let it come forth under the action and the power of the Holy Ghost. Let Thy Word fall on good ground.

Bring wisdom, bring understanding, bring knowledge and power to receive Thine engrafted Word to those that are listening this day. Let faith rise in the hearts of those that are hearing, those that are listening. Let the ear be sanctified to hear, let the eyes be sanctified to see, let the heart be sanctified to receive by Thy Spirit, O God, in Jesus' name.

Thy Word is power, bring deliverance in Thy power through Thy Word, Lord, Thy spoken Word and Thy written Word. O Lord God, show Thyself mighty on the behalf of those that are preparing to meet You in the air. Bless Your people this day and those that are yet in the valley of decision, help them to make the right decision and come quickly to You before the wrath of God be poured out upon this earth and bind the forces of hell that would seek to rob and thwart the Word of God from coming forth or being received.

In the name of Jesus Christ, let Your blood prevail this day, the blood of Jesus. Let it cover the minds of the listeners and the hearts, we pray, to Thy glory, Father, in Jesus' name, amen and amen.

Let me back up to the third chapter of 1st Thessalonians, the latter part of the third chapter, beginning at verse 11.

> *Now God himself and our Father, and our Lord Jesus Christ, direct our way unto you. And the Lord make you to increase and abound in love one toward another, and toward all men, even as we do toward you: to the end he may stablish your hearts unblameable in holiness before God, even our Father, at the coming of our Lord Jesus Christ with all his saints.*

Jesus is coming to this earth with all His saints.

> *Furthermore then we beseech you, brethren, and exhort you by the Lord Jesus, that as ye have received of us how ye ought to walk and to please God, so ye would abound more and more.*

That means grow greater in your knowledge of how you should walk unto all pleasing before the Almighty God.

> *For ye know what commandments we gave you by the Lord Jesus. For this is the will of God, even your sanctification, that ye should abstain from fornication:*

Hallelujah.

> *that every one of you should know how to possess his vessel in sanctification and honour; not in the lust of concupiscence, even as the Gentiles which*

know not God: that no man go beyond and defraud
his brother in any matter: because that the
Lord is the avenger of all such,

The Lord is, you see,

as we also have forewarned you and testified. For
God hath not called us unto uncleanness, but unto
holiness. He therefore that despiseth, despiseth not
man, but God, who hath also given unto us his holy
Spirit. But as touching brotherly love ye need not
that I write unto you: for ye yourselves are taught of
God to love one another. And indeed ye do it toward
all the brethren which are in all Macedonia: but we
beseech you, brethren, that you increase more and
more,

See, we grow in love more and more like we grow in
everything else that is of God.

and that ye study to be quiet, and to do your own
business,

Mind your own business, do your business, take care of
your own business,

and to work with your own hands, as we
commanded you; that ye may walk honestly toward
them that are without, and that ye may have lack of
nothing.

But I would not have you to be ignorant, brethren,
concerning them which are asleep, that ye sorrow
not, even as others which have no hope. For if we
believe that Jesus died and rose again, even so them
also which sleep in Jesus will God bring with him.

…will God bring with Him, the Lord God Jesus bring with Him.

> *For this we say unto you by the word of the Lord, that we which are alive and remain unto the coming of the Lord shall not prevent them which are asleep.*

those that have fallen asleep or have died in Christ.

> *For the Lord himself shall descend from heaven with a shout, with the voice of the archangel, and with the trump of God: and the dead in Christ shall rise first: then we which are alive and remain shall be caught up together with them in the clouds, to meet the Lord in the air: and so shall we ever be with the Lord. Wherefore comfort one another with these words.*

> *But of the times and the seasons, brethren, ye have no need that I write unto you. For yourselves know perfectly that the day of the Lord so cometh as a thief in the night. For when they shall say, Peace and safety; then sudden destruction cometh upon them, as travail upon a woman with child; and they shall not escape.*

Now a woman with child, heavy with child, a woman that is about to give birth, may know a date, a given date that her gynecologist may give her, but the very moment she's not aware if it's to happen naturally, you see, but she knows that she is heavy with child and that child's time to be born is near. So it is with the bride of Christ.

We do not know the moment nor the hour that Jesus Christ is to appear, but we can see by the things that our Lord and

Savior has taught us when he was here on earth 2,000 years ago. We can see that the coming of the Lord is near, so we are preparing.

We're in readiness, we're seeking in his face. And this is why he goes on to say, Paul goes on to say, let me read verse three again.

> *For when they shall say, Peace and safety; then sudden destruction cometh upon them, as travail upon a woman with child; and they shall not escape. But ye, brethren, are not in darkness, that that day should overtake you as a thief.*

When Jesus comes… we'll know it, because we will go up with him. He's not going to overtake us as a thief because he's already given us the signs to watch for his coming. He said, when we see these things, what we're looking upon today, he told us to look up for our redemption draweth nigh. Jesus is coming to redeem us out of this world.

Hallelujah. He said,

> *Ye are all the children of light, and the children of the day: we are not of the night, nor of darkness.*

Jesus is that day star. Hallelujah. He's that burning light unto those that are looking for him. And he gives us to walk in that glorious light. Spiritually, we're walking in Jesus unto heaven. Glory, Hallelujah!

For he's that glorious bright light shining in the souls of those that have been born again, redeemed by his spirit, washed in his blood and are looking for his coming. He said, we are not of the children of the night nor of darkness.

The devil is the prince of darkness. He abides in darkness and in great secrecy. He abides in lies because he is the father of lies. And all that will follow him have dark minds and dark hearts, just like satan.

But the word of God says, we are not like those that follow satan. We are children of the day and we abide in the light.

> *Ye are all the children of light, and the children of the day: we are not of the night, nor of darkness. Therefore let us not sleep, as do others;*

Do not be blind and walk around in a deep sleep as if you don't know what time it is and what day it is. Hallelujah.

> *we are not of the night, nor of darkness. Therefore let us not sleep, as do others; but let us watch and be sober.*

Let us watch! Keep watching, keep our eyes upon the Lord Jesus Christ. How? By his spirit. The Holy Spirit shows us, He takes the things that Christ has spoken and He reveals them to us. He gives us greater understanding as to what is on the heart of God the Father and God the Son.

He takes those glorious, precious mysteries of the kingdom and reveals them unto us, the children of day, the children of light. And therefore, we walk in the wisdom of God. We walk in the knowledge and the power of God. We walk with understanding and we know what to watch for. Hallelujah.

He said,

> *For they that sleep, sleep in the night; and they that be drunken are drunken in the night.*

It can be a bright day, but yet it's night to multitudes because they do not know the light, Jesus Christ, the light of the world.

> *But let us, who are of the day, be sober, putting on the breastplate of faith and love; and for an helmet, the hope of salvation. For God hath not appointed us to wrath,*

He's talking to the body of Christ and all those that will come to know Jesus Christ and will make haste to do it.

> *For God hath not appointed us to wrath, but to obtain salvation by our Lord Jesus Christ, who died for us, that, whether we wake or sleep, we should live together with him.*

Whether we are alive or passed on, we should live together with him. He's coming for us.

> *Wherefore comfort yourselves together, and edify one another, even as also ye do.*

Encourage one another to live holy, to live righteously, to fear God, to tremble at his word, to make preparations daily, to look for the coming of the Lord and to watch our own spirits, watch our hearts. Guard our hearts with the word of God. Comfort one another in these things. Encourage one another. That's what it means to edify one another. Build them up. Encourage them to look for the coming of the Lord.

No, you're not being over-religious. You're encouraging the hearts to get out of here. And the only way souls will escape the tribulation, the damnation that's coming upon this world is to be watching with readiness of heart, living holy, living sanctified, living separated from this world and the evils of this world, the sins and the lust of this world.

> *And we beseech you, brethren, to know them which labour among you, and are over you in the Lord, and admonish you; and to esteem them very highly in love for their work's sake.*

The Lord tells us to esteem them very highly in love for their work's sake and be at peace among yourselves. Thank God for putting that there.

> *And be at peace among yourselves.*

Because the devil is desiring to destroy the church. He cannot do it. He may be able to creep in and use those that are sitting in the church, but he cannot destroy the church of the Lord Jesus Christ because we are not a building.

We're souls in sanctified bodies which are to be glorified when Jesus comes. And he tells us,

> *Now we exhort you, brethren, warn them that are unruly, comfort the feebleminded, support the weak, be patient toward all men.*

This is what we are called to do. Watching for souls of men, warn them that are unruly, comfort the feeble-minded, those that may seem to be feeble, comfort them, support the weak, undergird them with love and the power of God's word.

> *be patient toward all men. See that none render evil for evil unto any man;*

And a lot of this is going on amongst Christians so-called, rendering evil for evil, it's wrong. It should not be. Someone do you evil, bend your knees, go be a tattletale, go straight to God and tell him everything that was said and done to you. God will take care of it. And then when you tell it, let it go… Let it go!

God will take care of it. He knows how to convict men by his spirit. Let him do the job. And if they won't yield to the chastening of God, if they will not be corrected, then count them as enemies. But still, love God. You have to love everyone no matter what's been done to you, you've got to love and forgive. Hallelujah. You don't have to be around a person holding them in your bosom to love.

God taught me that. We can love our enemies long distance and pray for them. Perhaps some will gather up the loins of their mind and sober up and realize where they are and come running to Jesus Christ, seeking his forgiveness.

And they have to ask yours if they've sinned against you. That's the way of the Lord. It's called righteousness, doing that which is right in the eyes of God.

> *See that none render evil for evil unto any man; but ever follow that which is good, both among yourselves, and to all men. Rejoice evermore. Pray without ceasing. In every thing give thanks: for this is the will of God in Christ Jesus concerning you. Quench not the Spirit.*

If the spirit of God is moving upon you, give him the right away. Don't try to stop his move because he's the one that is going to present you faultless when Jesus appears in the air for you.

> *Despise not prophesyings.*

There's a whole lot of prophesying going on, but true prophecy will tell you what is on God's heart concerning his children and will tell you, the children, what God desires.

Prove all things;

Test it out by the Word, not by your own understanding, but by the Word and power of God.

hold fast that which is good. Abstain from all appearance of evil. And the very God of peace sanctify you wholly;

W-H-O-L-L-Y, that means completely. He will do it if you obey what is given here. These are instructions and the wise will take heed to the instructions of the Lord.

and I pray God your whole spirit and soul and body be preserved blameless unto the coming of our Lord Jesus Christ. Faithful is he that calleth you, who also will do it.

He'll do it. you must yield. Don't quench the spirit. Hallelujah. And he says in verse 27,

I charge you by the Lord that this epistle be read unto all the holy brethren,

To everyone. Now, this is a condition that the bride of Christ will be when Jesus comes to gather the elect from all the earth. There is a prepared people watching, praying, waiting, seeking God, holding on, holding fast and not letting go.

They're not the ones that says, oh, the Lord delayeth his coming and start doing despiteful and wicked and evil things and yielding their bodies to fornication. No, our bodies are preserved as the temple of the Holy Spirit. And we must walk holy in mind, soul, spirit and body blameless before the Lord Jesus Christ.

He's coming for his bride to take us out of this world before tribulation hits. And God willing, next week, we're going into the book of Revelation and we're going to show you when the bride is out of here, what the tribulation period will be like. God, help the church of Jesus Christ to prepare for his coming.

May the Lord watch over you and you yield to the Holy Spirit in Jesus mighty name. Amen and amen.

The Stage is Set

Glory to God, we praise and honor the Lord today because of his goodness and his manifold blessings that he bestowed upon us. We honor the Most High God for his faithfulness and for his great love unto the children of men worldwide. God loves humanity, God loves the souls of men. And the truth that is given to us will show us that.

We've been speaking for about seven Sundays, including today, concerning the day of the Lord. The day that the Lord will come back to this earth, not to rapture the church, the bride of Christ, but to manifest his wrath and his indignation against the inhabitants of the earth for coming against his children, his people called the Jews. The Lord made a covenant with Abraham, Abram at the time, and then he renamed him Abraham because he was a friend of God and he still is.

And because of his faithfulness and his obedience to God's purpose and plan for his life and for humanity, God chose Abraham to be the father of faith. And because of his faith and his righteousness that God said that he was righteous because of his obedience to God, he was made righteous. So it is with those that believe on the Lord God Almighty and in the Godhead body today.

The Lord is coming and what we have seen and what we have witnessed by the way of television and radio and newspapers, it's just a taste of what will be during the terrible tribulation period that is coming upon the face of the earth when the bride of Christ is taken out of this world... Jesus is coming. In our last broadcast, we ministered from 1st Thessalonians chapters 4 and 5. The Lord wants his body prepared to meet him in the air.

Things that have been spoken of by the prophets of old are rapidly being fulfilled before our eyes daily, giving us to know that when we see these things come to pass, the Word of God says, look up for your redemption draweth nigh. We are going to be redeemed completely out of this world to be in the presence of God Almighty and the Son, Jesus Christ, who is the bridegroom of the bride, the church of Jesus Christ in this earth. After, immediately after we are taken out of here, in the 12th chapter of Revelation, I want you to see what the devil is truly like.

The Word of God says,

> And there appeared a great wonder in heaven; a woman clothed with the sun, and the moon under her feet, and upon her head a crown of twelve stars: and she being with child cried, travailing in birth, and pained to be delivered. And there appeared another wonder in heaven; and behold a great red dragon, having seven heads and ten horns, and seven crowns upon his heads.

> And his tail drew the third part of the stars of heaven, and did cast them to the earth: and the dragon stood before the woman which was ready to be delivered, for to devour her child as soon as it was born. And she brought forth a man child, who was to rule all nations with a rod of iron:

This man-child is Jesus Christ.

> and her child was caught up unto God, and to his throne.

Jesus has gone back to be with the Father. He sits now at the right-hand side of the Father, on the throne of God, his Father, making intercessions for us today, watching over from heaven the affairs of the earth, watching the timetable in the earth. And he says,

> *And the woman fled into the wilderness, where she hath a place prepared of God, that they should feed her there a thousand two hundred and threescore days.*

Let us pray:

Our Father which art in heaven, hallowed be thy name. Thy kingdom come, thy will be done on earth as it is in heaven. And give us this day our daily bread. Forgive us our debts, as we forgive those that are indebted to us. Lead us not into temptation, but deliver us from evil. For thine is the kingdom and the power and the glory forever.

Have your mighty way. You're the God of the universe. You're the God of all creation. You're the God of all mankind. You're the God that knows the end from the beginning. And when time is over, you will still be God almighty. You will still be that glorious and mighty one. Hallelujah. Bless your mighty name today.

We give honor to your name. Take charge right now over the hearts and minds of every listener. And let your name be glorified. Let your truth prevail this day. Let truth prevail in the earth. Let truth prevail over the wicked one.

Hallelujah. You're the God of truth, the God of light. You're the God of mercy. And you're the God of vengeance.

Let your truth come forth this day under the unction and the power of the Holy Ghost and penetrate the darkness that's in the minds and the hearts of many. And encourage those that are looking and preparing for your coming, your return, to gather the elect unto thyself.

Be glorified. Hallelujah. Raise up, Lord, those that are cast down this day. Put hope and joy and expectancy in the heart of those that have grown faint. Let thy strength be poured within, thy might be poured within thy children this day. And let hope arise higher than ever, greater than ever.

Be glorified. And let the church of Jesus Christ be prepared to meet you without spot and without blemish. In Jesus' name we pray.

Gather the souls in that are lost. Those that sit in darkness, let them see this glorious light shining as the Holy Spirit reveals thy son. When he reveals this great redemption that can come only through Jesus Christ.

Let many that sit in darkness see this great light and forsake every way and come unto you and be saved and be delivered. In Jesus' name we plead the blood of Jesus. Let your blood wash whiter than snow this day.

Gather unto thyself all that are to make the rapture. In Jesus' name. Amen and Amen.

Verse 7 of Revelations 12,

> *And there was war in heaven: Michael and his angels fought against the dragon; and the dragon fought and his angels, and prevailed not; neither was their place found any more in heaven.*

Satan cast out, no more that glorious anointed cherub, no longer in the power of God but cast out to the earth. No longer that beautiful glorious angel that was created holy. He's just the opposite.

> *And the great dragon was cast out, that old serpent, called the Devil, and Satan, which deceiveth*

Not deceived… he's yet deceiving

> *the whole world. He was cast out into the earth*

and believe me he's here today. Not glorying in him but acknowledging that he's here.

> *And I heard a loud voice saying in heaven, Now is come salvation, and strength, and the kingdom of our God, and the power of his Christ: for the accuser of our brethren is cast down, which accused them before our God day and night. And they*

the brethren

> *overcame him by the blood of the lamb and by the word of their testimony. And they loved not their lives unto the death and they overcame him.*

God has given us his overcoming power. He's given us his mighty victory. He's given us to be more than conquerors through Jesus Christ that loved us from the beginning. God has given us power.

Every true believer has power over the devil and his angels or his demons. He is no longer Lucifer his name is called the destroyer, Satan, the deceiver, the evil one, the dragon, Apollyon, the serpent. He's all of these things, he's also called the accuser because he likes to be in the presence of God and accuse the brethren of their weakness or their failure to obey God. But listen in verse 11,

And they overcame him by the blood of the Lamb,

We are to plead the blood of Jesus. We are to abide under the blood of Jesus. We are to live under the anointing of the blood. There's power in the blood, there's life in the blood, we live because of the blood of Jesus. Not of bulls and rams, hallelujah, but of Jesus, of Jesus, the Lamb of God... the Lamb that came from heaven.

They overcame him by the blood of the lamb and by the word of their testimony.

We have a testimony in the earth true to Christ, true to Christ, no matter what, true to the living word

and they love not their lives unto the death.

Many are selling out because they love this present world. They will not suffer reproach or persecution or troubles.

Everybody's telling you God is good and God is, I'm the first one to say, but there are things that we have to go through because we're in an earthly tabernacle. And we have to learn Christ.

Christ learned obedience through the things that he suffered and we are also going to learn obedience through things that comes against us. And we love not our lives unto the death, even if we have to die. Many have died, look in the 11th chapter of Hebrews, I call it the faith chapter.

And there have been many after them, even up to this present time, that have died for the sake, for the cause of Christ, loving not their lives, not betraying the Lord Jesus Christ or turning against him.

Many have given up because of the things that they have gone through. Many have allowed their hearts to become hardened and accused the Lord God falsely. But remember, Satan is in this world. he's the one that's doing these wicked things. He's the one that is causing famine and death and destruction and so forth. It is the enemy that's in this world, fighting against the souls, fighting against the people of God, the creation of God in the form of human flesh.

> *Therefore rejoice, ye heavens, and ye that dwell in them. Woe to the inhabiters of the earth and of the sea! for the devil is come down unto you, having great wrath, because he knoweth that he hath but a short time.*
>
> *And when the dragon saw that he was cast unto the earth, he persecuted the woman which brought forth the man child.*

Remember how Jesus, Mary and Joseph had to take Jesus into Egypt because the devil was killing the little ones, two years old and under?

> *And to the woman were given two wings of a great eagle, that she might fly into the wilderness, into her place, where she is nourished for a time, and times, and half a time, from the face of the serpent. And the serpent cast out of his mouth water as a flood after the woman, that he might cause her to be carried away of the flood.*

You see, he's the destroyer. He's the one that brings destruction.

> *And the earth helped the woman, and the earth opened her mouth, and swallowed up the flood which the dragon cast out of his mouth. And the dragon was wroth with the woman, and went to*

make war with the remnant of her seed, which keep the commandments of God,

which keep the commandments of God,

and have the testimony of Jesus Christ.

We are to love the Lord our God, that commandment has never stopped. It is still in effect today with all our heart, with all our soul, with all our mind, with all our strength and our neighbor as ourselves. This is the commandment, or these are the commandments of God. And Jesus said, on these two hang all the law and the prophets.

And I stood upon the sand of the sea, and saw a beast rise up out of the sea, having seven heads and ten horns,

You see, because the Lord has caused the woman to go and rest in the presence of the Most High. And this is what will happen after the church is taken out.

And I stood upon the sand of the sea, and saw a beast rise up out of the sea, having seven heads and ten horns, and upon his horns ten crowns, and upon his heads the name of blasphemy. And the beast which I saw was like unto a leopard, and his feet were as the feet of a bear, and his mouth as the mouth of a lion: and the dragon gave him his power, and his seat, and great authority. And I saw one of his heads as it were wounded to death; and his deadly wound was healed: and all the world wondered after the beast.

They wondered in awe and admiration. All the world, not the bride, because the bride is out of this world at this point.

And they worshiped the dragon which gave power unto the beast.

> *And they worshipped the dragon which gave power unto the beast: and they worshipped the beast, saying, Who is like unto the beast? who is able to make war with him? And there was given unto him a mouth speaking great things and blasphemies;*

Heresies, falsehood, ugly things.

> *and power was given unto him to continue forty and two months.*

three and a half years. And he's going to use those first three and a half years to deceive the whole world.

> *And he opened his mouth in blasphemy against God, to blaspheme his name, and his tabernacle, and them that dwell in heaven.*

He's going to speak evil of heaven and all that dwell therein because see, he's still angry. He's still full of wrath because he's been cast out. And this is how he's going to try to get back at God to devour and deceive the whole world. Let me read verse six again.

> *And he opened his mouth in blasphemy against God, to blaspheme his name, and his tabernacle, and them that dwell in heaven. And it was given unto him to make war with the saints,*

those that were left here to go through the tribulation period because they were not ready to meet Jesus in the air. Yes, there are going to be many Christians left here, lukewarm Christians, carnal-minded Christians, Christians that are making this world their home without Christ.

There are going to be many left and many will go through that great tribulation period and many will awake out of their deep sleep and put on the Lord. They will come after him with a whole heart. And yes, the church, the bride will already be out of here.

This is why the Lord is telling us to be children, walk as children of the day and not of the night, to be sober and to watch for his coming, but many are not. It amazes me, many are so close to the coming of the Lord and are yet going to miss heaven. They're going to miss being taken out of here and will have to go through the great tribulation period.

> *And it was given unto him to make war with the saints, and to overcome them: and power was given him over all kindreds, and tongues, and nations. And all that dwell upon the earth shall worship him, whose names are not written in the book of life of the Lamb slain from the foundation of the world.*

Get busy, get busy, precious hearts. Get your name written in the Lamb's book of life and do not forsake to follow the Lord. Be true to yourselves as well as God.

> *If any man have an ear, let him hear. He that leadeth into captivity shall go into captivity: he that killeth with the sword must be killed with the sword. Here is the patience and the faith of the saints.*

God is telling many to get ready, to escape these things and many will be left here. And the Lord said, here is the patience, you see, and the faith of the saints that are left here.

> *And I beheld another beast coming up out of the earth; and he had two horns like a lamb, and he spake as a dragon. And he exerciseth all the power of the first beast before him, and causeth the earth and them which dwell therein to worship the first beast, whose deadly wound was healed.*

You see, the devil has power to heal. You understand this? He's going to work many diabolical wonders

> *And he doeth great wonders, so that he maketh fire come down from heaven on the earth in the sight of men, and deceiveth them that dwell on the earth by the means of those miracles which he had power to do in the sight of the beast; saying to them that dwell on the earth, that they should make an image to the beast, which had the wound by a sword, and did live. And he had power to give life unto the image of the beast,*

See this is great, great and marvelous diabolical miracles. And it's going to all be done by witchcraft, great sorceries. This is why we see it's so plentiful in the world today and in our nation that is supposed to have intelligence, but it's the so-called intelligent ones that have been delving into the powers of darkness and boldly declare it so. The devil is setting up his kingdom to work these diabolical miracles.

> *And he had power to give life unto the image of the beast, that the image of the beast should both speak, and cause that as many as would not worship the image of the beast should be killed.*

And he causeth all, both small and great, rich and poor, free and bond, to receive a mark in their right hand, or in their foreheads: and that no man might buy or sell, save he that had the mark, or the name of the beast, or the number of his name.

Here is wisdom. Let him that hath understanding count the number of the beast: for it is the number of a man; and his number is Six hundred threescore and six.

And this is why God is declaring to us his truth. God is preaching. God is anointing his servants worldwide to speak these things that you hear me speaking because God wants his people saved and delivered out of this world. In Jesus name come and be made whole. Amen and amen.

Be Ye Holy

Greetings to everyone of you in the name of our Lord and Savior Jesus Christ, with great joy and peace, I come to you in the authority of the name of Jesus. We thank God for the opportunity that He's been giving us weekly to come your way and to present unto you a series titled The Day of the Lord. The Day of the Lord will be one great day when Jesus Christ comes back to this earth to do the will of God the Father, amen to set in order all rule under His authority and under His dominion. Praise His holy name. We thank God for Jesus Christ, the Son of the Living God, the Savior of all the world, the mighty Deliverer. Amen.

God loves the souls of men and he manifested his love in the person of his Son, Christ Jesus. And this love is going around the world to save that which is lost. This invitation to come unto him and be saved is given unto all mankind everywhere.

Everyone will not receive the invitation, nor will they answer the one that sent the invitation, but still it is given. The doors of God's mercies will soon be closing to many. And the word of God must be revealed, it must be preached uncompromisingly.

The Lord revealed to me, we were talking this morning before coming to church with certain ones and we were talking about the compromises that man makes, Christians and ministers of the gospel of Jesus Christ, make with the world and with those that are worldly coming into the house of the Lord. And the Spirit of God spoke to me and said, we must pray and bind the spirit of compromise.

Little did I even have even thought to think that to compromise is actually yielding to a spirit sent by the devil to cause true Christians to compromise the word of God. We cannot afford to do it, precious ones. We cannot afford to yield our mind to anything but God himself, the Godhead body.

Amen. And we know that Jesus Christ, the Son of God is the word of life. Hallelujah.

He's the living word, He's the bread come down from heaven in every word that has proceeded out of his mouth. We must live by, uncompromisingly with ourselves or anyone else. The love of God is so great, but he does not compromise. He delivers and sanctify. Bless His holy name. And we must be like him at his appearing. And it takes courage. It takes pure love and true holiness to live an uncompromising life before the Lord and before humanity. But we must do it by the grace and power of the Lord Jesus Christ. Amen.

Let us pray,

Precious Father, we thank you for the opportunity you've given us once more and again to be on the air. And Lord, we're asking that you would reach your people by the word of life indeed. Cause your people to hear and understand, remove dullness, remove blindness, unstop the deaf ears, melt the hardened hearts that your word may penetrate and destroy darkness and bring your glorious light and thy great salvation within the innermost being.

Thy kingdom come, thy will be done on earth as it is in heaven. And show forth the greatness of your power by bringing deliverance to the captives and the receiving of sight to the blind that no heart will be able to accuse you,

Lord. You will warn every man, every woman, boy and girl of thy great riches and of thy kingdom.

You will warn, Lord. Not only will you invite, but you will warn those that will rebel against you. Thy will be done this day through the reading of your word, In Jesus' name we pray. Amen and amen.

Matthew chapter 23, we will go in today and I want to read straight through.

I want you to hear what the Lord Jesus Christ contended with and is yet contending with today. And from there we will go to Romans chapter 11, God willing.

Chapter 23 of Saint Matthew,

> *Then spake Jesus to the multitude, and to his disciples, saying, The scribes and the Pharisees sit in Moses' seat: all therefore whatsoever they bid you observe, that observe and do; but do not ye after their works: for they say, and do not. For they bind heavy burdens and grievous to be borne, and lay them on men's shoulders; but they themselves will not move them with one of their fingers.*

They told you what to do, but they won't do the work themselves.

> *But all their works they do for to be seen of men: they make broad their phylacteries, and enlarge the borders of their garments, and love the uppermost rooms at feasts, and the chief seats in the*

*synagogues, and greetings in the markets, and to be
called of men, Rabbi, Rabbi. But be not ye called
Rabbi: for one is your Master, even Christ; and all
ye are brethren. And call no man your father upon
the earth: for one is your Father, which is in
heaven. Neither be ye called masters: for one is
your Master, even Christ.*

He speaks it again.

*But he that is greatest among you shall be your
servant.*

The one that is greatest among you shall be your servant,
not you serving them.

And whosoever shall exalt himself shall be abased.

These are the words of Jesus Christ.

And he that shall humble himself shall be exalted.

Do that work that others won't do. Humble yourself and do
it. And to God be the glory, God will exalt you.

*But woe unto you, scribes and Pharisees,
hypocrites! for ye shut up the kingdom of heaven
against men: for ye neither go in yourselves, neither
suffer ye them that are entering to go in.*

Those that would enter in you're blocking them, you will
not allow them.

*Woe unto you, scribes and Pharisees, hypocrites!
for ye devour widows' houses, and for a pretence
make long prayer: therefore ye shall receive the
greater damnation.*

Woe unto you, scribes and Pharisees, hypocrites!
for ye compass sea and land to make one proselyte,
and when he is made, ye make him twofold more the
child of hell than yourselves.

Hear what Jesus is saying.

Woe unto you, ye blind guides, which say,
Whosoever shall swear by the temple, it is nothing;
but whosoever shall swear by the gold of the temple,
he is a debtor! Ye fools and blind:

You mean to tell me Jesus would say that? He said it.

Ye fools and blind: for whether is greater, the gold,
or the temple that sanctifieth the gold? And,
Whosoever shall swear by the altar, it is nothing;
but whosoever sweareth by the gift that is upon it,
he is guilty. Ye fools and blind:

That means blind to the will of God, blind to the knowledge
of God.

for whether is greater, the gift, or the altar that
sanctifieth the gift? Whoso therefore shall swear by
the altar, sweareth by it, and by all things thereon.

everything that is on the altar, you swear by it also.

And whoso shall swear by the temple, sweareth by
it, and by him that dwelleth therein. And he that
shall swear by heaven, sweareth by the throne of
God, and by him that sitteth thereon.

That's why Jesus tells us in the Beatitudes not to swear by
anything. We're not to swear. Even when you go into court,
do not swear. Do you swear to tell the truth? Say, no, I will

affirm. I will not swear. Be strong in the Lord. Be strong in the Lord. See, this is compromise.

Jesus said,

> *And he that shall swear by heaven, sweareth by the throne of God, and by him that sitteth thereon.*
>
> *Woe unto you, scribes and Pharisees, hypocrites! for ye pay tithe of mint and anise and cummin, and have omitted the weightier matters of the law, judgment, mercy, and faith: these ought ye to have done, and not to leave the other undone.*

In other words, continue to pay tithe, but show true judgment. Judge ye what is right. Do it, show mercy, manifest the faith of God.

He said,

> *Ye blind guides, which strain at a gnat, and swallow a camel. Woe unto you, scribes and Pharisees, hypocrites! for ye make clean the outside of the cup and of the platter, but within they are full of extortion and excess. Thou blind Pharisee, cleanse first that which is within the cup and platter, that the outside of them may be clean also.*
>
> *Woe unto you, scribes and Pharisees, hypocrites! for ye are like unto whited sepulchres, which indeed appear beautiful outward, but are within full of dead men's bones, and of all uncleanness.*

Boy, when God, I hear many people say, God doesn't look on the outer appearance, he looks at the heart. Yes, he does and what he is saying, what he sees in the heart, he's describing right here. And he has every right to do because he knows what's in the heart.

> *Even so ye also outwardly appear righteous unto men, but within ye are full of hypocrisy and iniquity.*

The Lord Jesus calling it for what it is, what he has seen and witnessed in the heart of man, leaders.

> *Woe unto you, scribes and Pharisees, hypocrites! because ye build the tombs of the prophets, and garnish the sepulchres of the righteous, and say, If we had been in the days of our fathers, we would not have been partakers with them in the blood of the prophets.*

In other words, we would not have killed them, had we been back there, we would not have destroyed them.

And here's what Jesus says,

> *Wherefore ye be witnesses unto yourselves, that ye are the children of them which killed the prophets. Fill ye up then the measure of your fathers. Ye serpents,*

You mean Jesus Christ goes around calling people serpents? Here it is. (someone may say) I'm no serpent, that's not right that's not grace, that's not love to call me out of my name... Jesus describes a person by their names.

> *Ye serpents, ye generation of vipers, how can ye escape the damnation of hell?*

Whoa, this is tough.

Wherefore behold, I send unto you prophets and wise men and scribes.

> *Wherefore, behold, I send unto you prophets, and wise men, and scribes: and some of them ye shall kill and crucify; and some of them shall ye scourge in your synagogues, and persecute them from city to city:*

Why? They hate what God has to say. The scribe writes down what God says. The prophet speaks thus, saith the Lord. You understand? And the righteous, the wise are aware of the mind of Christ and they make it known.

And the world, the church world hates it. Don't speak to us these things. Speak to us smooth things. We don't want to hear that. You're to exalt the people. Prophecy is to prophesize, to exalt the people. Prophesy what thus saith the Lord. And if a humble hearer thereof, you will be exalted. Glory, Hallelujah.

Let me read this again.

> *Wherefore, behold, I send unto you prophets, and wise men, and scribes: and some of them ye shall kill and crucify; and some of them shall ye scourge in your synagogues, and persecute them from city to city: that upon you may come all the righteous blood shed upon the earth*

upon you, you that will do these things that will speak evil of the dignities of God and the mind of the Lord. The Lord said upon you shall come the blood of all those that have been killed for the will of God.

*that upon you may come all the righteous blood
shed upon the earth, from the blood of righteous
Abel unto the blood of Zacharias son of Barachias,
whom ye slew between the temple and the
altar. Verily I say unto you, All these things shall
come upon this generation.*

Glory to God. People wonder why… so many things. Let's go to the Word, find out why.

*O Jerusalem, Jerusalem, thou that killest the
prophets, and stonest them which are sent unto thee,
how often would I have gathered thy children
together, even as a hen gathereth her chickens
under her wings, and ye would not!*

I would have preserved you. I would have brought you in closer. I would have been your covering. I would have protected you.

*Behold, your house is left unto you desolate. For I
say unto you, Ye shall not see me henceforth, till ye
shall say, Blessed is he that cometh in the name of
the Lord.*

And they shall say, blessed is he that cometh in the name of the Lord, because he is coming. In Romans 11,

*I say then, Hath God cast away his people? God
forbid. For I also am an Israelite, of the seed of
Abraham, of the tribe of Benjamin. God hath not
cast away his people which he foreknew. Wot ye not
what the scripture saith of Elias? how he maketh
intercession to God against Israel, saying, Lord,
they have killed thy prophets, and digged down*

thine altars; and I am left alone, and they seek my life.

This is what Elijah said.

But what saith the answer of God unto him?

This is what God answered him.

I have reserved to myself seven thousand men, who have not bowed the knee to the image of Baal. Even so then at this present time also there is a remnant according to the election of grace. And if by grace, then is it no more of works:

otherwise grace is no more grace. But if it be of works, then is it no more grace: otherwise work is no more work. What then? Israel hath not obtained that which he seeketh for; but the election hath obtained it, and the rest were blinded

Why? Because they forsook the truth. Jesus came unto his own, and his own received him not, but as many as received him, to them gave he eternal life. As many as believe on his name, whether they be Jew, Greek, or Gentile.

(according as it is written, God hath given them the spirit of slumber, eyes that they should not see, and ears that they should not hear;) unto this day. And David saith, Let their table be made a snare, and a trap, And a stumblingblock, and a recompence unto them:

Let their eyes be darkened, that they may not see, And bow down their back alway. I say then, Have they stumbled that they should fall? God forbid:

but rather through their fall salvation is come unto
the Gentiles, for to provoke them to jealousy.

This is why God allowed it to happen, to provoke them to
jealousy. When they see the glorious favor that God has
bestowed upon the Gentiles. Many are saved today because
of the blindness of some. He says,

Now if the fall of them be the riches of the world,
and the diminishing of them the riches of the
Gentiles; how much more their fulness?

When they come back to God,

For I speak to you Gentiles, inasmuch as I am the
apostle of the Gentiles, I magnify mine office:

I'm happy. I'm just happy to be an apostle to the Gentiles.

If by any means I may provoke to immolation them
which are my flesh,

my kinfolk,

I might save some of them. For if the casting away
of them be the reconciling of the world,
what shall the receiving of them be, but life from the
dead?

God shall resurrect his own. Hallelujah. God will deliver
Israel. They will see, their understanding will come back,
their eyes will be open, their ears will be open, their hearts
will be open to know the Messiah. And they shall say,
blessed is he that cometh in the name of the Lord. It shall
happen. Glory be to God. He said,

for if the first fruit be holy,

meaning the Israelites,

the lump is also holy.

Get this?

And if the root be holy, so are the branches. And if some of the branches be broken off,

meaning some will not receive Christ as Messiah ever,

and thou being a wild olive tree,

talking to us Gentiles,

wild olive tree, grafted in among them,

the Lord blended us in as the seed of Abraham, children of faith,

and with them partakers of the root and fatness of the olive tree.

Hallelujah.

Boast not against the branches. But if thou boast, thou bearest not the root, but the root thee. Thou wilt say then, The branches were broken off, that I might be graffed in. Well...

you're saying,

Well; because of unbelief they were broken off, and thou standest by faith. Be not highminded, but fear:

Be not high-minded. Love the Israelites, love them because they are God's natural olive branch. Hallelujah.

Be not highminded, but fear: for if God spared not the natural branches, take heed lest he also spare not thee

We have to have the right attitude. We have to have the right mind. We must be full of the love of the Lord God Almighty.

> *Behold therefore the goodness and severity of God: on them which fell, severity; but toward thee, goodness, if thou continue in his goodness:*

if thou continue in his goodness, that great big if.

> *otherwise thou also shalt be cut off. And they also, if they abide not still in unbelief, shall be graffed in:*

come back into their natural place, their rightful place.

> *For God is able to graft them in again,*

and not only is God able, he's going to do it.

> *For if thou wert cut out of the olive tree which is wild by nature, and wert graffed contrary to nature into a good olive tree: how much more shall these, which be the natural branches, be graffed into their own olive tree?*

> *For I would not, brethren, that ye should be ignorant of this mystery, lest ye should be wise in your own conceits; that blindness in part is happened to Israel, until the fulness of the Gentiles be come in.*

See, there's a set time for everything under the sun. Jesus Christ is the fulfillment of the law. Praise God. And those that have rejected Jesus are not abiding in grace. They are not abiding in life everlasting, but they will. Eyes will come open, God will save, God will deliver. Hallelujah. Some through the fire, some through great floods.

Hallelujah. Some through great rejection, but they are coming to find out that Jesus is indeed the Christ.

Praise the Lord of hosts.

Many have already, but as a whole, it shall happen. Let me read 25 again.

> *For I would not, brethren, that ye should be ignorant of this mystery, lest ye should be wise in your own conceits; that blindness in part is happened to Israel, until the fulness of the Gentiles be come in. And so all Israel shall be saved: as it is written, There shall come out of Sion the Deliverer, And shall turn away ungodliness from Jacob:*

Jesus is coming!

> *For this is my covenant unto them, When I shall take away their sins. As concerning the gospel, they are enemies for your sakes: but as touching the election, they are beloved for the fathers' sakes. For the gifts and calling of God are without repentance.*

> *For as ye in times past have not believed God, yet have now obtained mercy through their unbelief: even so have these also now not believed, that through your mercy they also may obtain mercy. For God hath concluded them all in unbelief, that he might have mercy upon all.*

So we that are enlightened, we that have known the mercies of God ought to pray them through. Pray for Israel.

Pray for the mighty eyes that God has put in them be opened and that they might receive the true counsel of God. Hallelujah. The fullness of Christ. Amen. Oh, the depth and the riches, both of the wisdom and knowledge of God is what the Lord desires to reveal unto you, his people. Amen and amen.

Liten to the Podcast

Listen to Evangelist Martha P. Davis today at your favorite podcast location. Look for God's Holy Mountain Broadcast in the following platforms:

Amazon: music.amazon.com/podcasts

Apple: podcasts.apple.com

Boom Play: boomplaymusic.com/podcasts

iHeart Radio: iheart.com/podcast

Instagram: instagram.com

Player FM: player.fm

Pod Chaser: podchaser.com

Podbean: ghmb.podbean.com/

Spotify: open.spotify.com

Youtube: youtube.com